Hugo's Simplified System

Spanish in Three Months

Isabel Cisneros

Hugo's Language Books Limited

This edition
© 1984 Hugo's Language Books Ltd
All rights reserved
ISBN 0 85285 065 4

8th impression 1993

Written by
Isabel Cisneros

Set in 10/12pt Plantin by
Phoenix Photosetting
Printed and Bound in Great Britain by
The Bath Press, Avon

Preface

This new edition of 'Spanish in Three Months' has been written for us by Isabel Cisneros, who has considerable experience in teaching her native tongue to sixth forms, adult beginners and more advanced students. The book is designed for people working without a teacher, who want to acquire a good working knowledge of Spanish in a short time. The grammar is presented concisely and clearly, maintaining the Hugo principle of teaching only what is really essential – and yet providing a complete course in written and conversational Spanish. Using this book together with the related cassette recordings which we have produced as optional extras (details sent upon request) will give a further dimension to your studies.

Ideally you should spend about an hour a day on the course (maybe a little less if you don't use the recordings), although there is not hard and fast rule on this. Do as much as you feel capable of doing; if you have no special aptitude for language-learning, there is no point in forcing yourself beyond your daily capacity to assimilate new material. It is much better to learn a little at a time, and to learn that thoroughly.

In studying the lessons, first read each rule or numbered section carefully and re-read it to ensure that you have fully understood the grammar and examples given. Try to understand rather than memorize; if you have understood, the exercises and drills will ensure that you remember the rules through applying them. Translate the exercises and check your answers against the key at the back of the book; the vocabularies in each lesson list those words not previously supplied elsewhere in the text. If you make mistakes and cannot understand why, go back to the relevant grammar section and read it again.

Having completed the written exercises, move on to the drills and speak both stimulus and response out aloud. Work through them line by line and use them as a test to see if you are ready to move on to the next lesson. In addition to the valuable oral practice in pronunciation and general fluency provided by these drills, they may also be treated as written exercises – answers are at the back of the book.

Each lesson finishes with a conversation in everyday Spanish, against which you will find an English translation. It is important to remember that idiomatic language cannot be translated word for word without the occasional appearance of some rather stilted phrases. These conversations should be read aloud until you can do so without hesitation; take careful note of the use of idioms and new vocabulary, as well as relating the constructions you hear to those you have just learnt.

The course is rounded off with a selection of reading passages taken from modern Spanish literature, which you should read and read again as soon as you feel able to do so without too much need to refer to the English translations. These will add to your comprehension of the written language, and will also give you a taste of the pleasures in store, should you decide to take your study of Spanish to a more advanced level.

When the course is completed, you should have a very good understanding of the language – more than sufficient for general holiday or business purposes, and enough to lead quickly into an examination syllabus if this is your eventual aim. Remember that it is important to continue expanding your vocabulary through reading, listening to the radio if possible, and best of all through visiting the country. We hope you will enjoy 'Spanish in Three Months', and wish you success with your studies.

Contents

The Spanish alphabet

This consists of 29 letters, of which K and W are found only in words taken from other languages. Note the letters CH, LL and Ñ: in Spanish dictionaries, words beginning with any one of these will be found after C, L and N. Below, we give the 'name' of each letter written according to our system of imitated pronunciation (explained on page 10).

A (ah)	F ('eff-ay)	L ('ell-ay)	P (pay)	V ('oo-vay)
B (bay)	G (Hay)	LL ('ell-yay)	Q (koo)	W ('oo-vay-'do-blay)
C (thay)	H ('ah-chay)	M ('emm-ay)	R ('airr-ay)	X ('ay-kiss)
CH (chay)	I (ee)	N ('enn-ay)	S ('ess-ay)	Y (ee-gre-'ay-gah)
D (day)	J ('Ho-tah)	Ñ ('enn-yay)	T (tay)	Z ('thay-tah)
E (ay)	K (kah)	O (o)	U (oo)	

Pronunciation

Before you start the first lesson, read the following rules and advice on pronunciation. There's no need to learn these rules by heart; refer back to them at frequent intervals and you will soon know them well. If you use our cassette recordings, everything will be made much clearer; these tapes enable you to hear the Spanish words and phrases at the same time as you read them. As Spanish is a very phonetic language, once you are familiar with its sounds you will always know how to pronounce the printed word.

Stress

In Spanish, the following rules apply:

a) Most words ending in a **vowel, n** or **s,** bear the stress on the *next to last* syllable: examen, flores, hombre, cigarrillo.

b) Most words ending in a **consonant** other than n or s, bear the stress on the *last* syllable: papel, ciudad, mujer, capital.

c) Exceptions to these two rules are indicated by a written accent on the stressed syllable: árbol, lámpara, estación, inglés, música.

d) The written accent is also used to distinguish words which have the same spelling but different meanings: el (the), él (he); si (if), sí (yes); mi (my), mí (me); mas (but), más (more).

e) The vowels **a, e** and **o** are strong vowels; **i** and **u** are weak ones. When two strong vowels come together, they are pronounced separately: paella, teatro, poeta.
When two weak vowels come together, the stress is on the last one: cuida, viuda.
When a strong vowel and a weak one come together, the strong vowel is stressed unless the weak one is accentuated: aire, jaula, oído, aún.

In our 'imitated pronunciation' (see page 10) we show which is the stressed syllable by marking ' in front of it.

Pronunciation of vowels

The Spanish vowels are **a, e, i, o** and **u**. Each vowel has only one sound; this is not quite so long and broad as the English equivalent given below. The vowel sounds are also shortened, as in other languages, when they occur in an unstressed word or syllable, or preceding a consonant.

a is pronounced like 'ah' in English: **al** (to), **la** (the), **casa** (house).

e is pronounced like 'ay': **me** (me), **de** (from), **le** (him).

i is pronounced like 'ee': **mi** (my), **prima** (first).

o is pronounced like 'o': **lo** (the), **no** (no), **gato** (cat).

u is pronounced like 'oo': **tu** (your), **su** (their), **uno** (one).

Pronunciation of consonants

There are only two Spanish consonants that are pronounced quite unlike their English counterparts: **z** and **j**. There are others which differ in various lesser ways. Note the following points:

z is pronounced like 'th' in 'month' or 'thick': **voz, luz, paz, vez, zapato**.

j is pronounced like the German guttural 'ch' as in 'auch', or like 'ch' in the Scottish 'loch'. This sound is merely the English 'h' pronounced in the throat: if you find it hard to make, simply pronounce it like an aspirated 'h': **ojo, jugar, juzgar, caja**.

ch is pronounced as in 'cheap' or 'much': **muchacha**.

c before **e** or **i** is pronounced like the Spanish z: **cena, cinco, once**.

g before **e** or **i** is pronounced like the Spanish j: **coger, general, gigante**.

g before any other letter is like 'g' in 'go': **gato**.

gu before **e** or **i** is like 'g' in 'go'; before any other vowel it is like 'gw' or 'goo': **guerra, guía**.

h is not pronounced at all: **hijo, hablar**.

ll is pronounced nearly like 'll' in 'million': **calle, silla, llamar.**

ñ is almost like 'ni' in 'companion': **niño, señor.**

qu is like 'k': **que, quince.**

r is rolled on the tip of the tongue more than in English, especially at the beginning of a word or syllable: **raro.**

s is always pronounced sharp, as in 'see' or 'last', never like a z as in 'easy' or 'miser': **casa, mesa.**

y is like 'y' in 'yes': **yo.** But alone or at the end of a word it is like the vowel i ('ee'): **y, soy.**

Varying pronunciations

The lisping pronunciation of **z**, and of **c** before **e** or **i,** is usual in Castile; as Castilian is considered the best Spanish, we recommend that you adopt this pronunciation in preference to any other variations you may hear. But in Central and South America (and in some parts of Spain) it is usual to pronounce z, and c before e or i, like the English 's'.

Many Spaniards pronounce the final **d** like 'th' in 'thin', 'myth'; some will pronounce **d** in the middle of a word like 'th' in 'then'. This you should avoid copying; remember to pronounce **madre** as ''mah-dray', not as ''mah-thray'. A final **d** should not be made too sharp or distinct.

It is also not unusual for Spaniards to confuse the sound of **b** with that of **v**, so that **vaca** sounds like 'baca', etc. This is not wrong, and the tape recordings of this course will illustrate it throughout – see page 29.

The letter **ll** is pronounced in several ways; we imitate it as l'y, but in some areas of Spain and in Latin America it has a strong guttural sound, with the 'l' virtually disappearing. In the Spanish province of Andalusia and in Argentina it is even stronger, the 'l' sound being replaced by something like a soft 'j' or the 'si' in 'occasion'. Thus, **mantilla** (which we imitate as mahn-'tee-l'yah) becomes mahn-'tee-yah or mahn-'tee-j'yah.

Punctuation signs and accents

Question marks and exclamation marks are placed at both ends of the phrase, the first one being inverted. The diaresis (¨) is placed over u when preceded by g, to show that the u must be pronounced: **agüero.** The tilde (˜) is placed over n, when that letter is to be pronounced like 'ni' in 'onion': **mañana.** The acute accent (´) is the only one used in Spanish, its use being explained on page 7. It never alters the pronunciation of a letter. It is also used in such words as **cúando** and **dónde** (when, where), when they actually ask a question: **¿Cuándo llega el buque?** (When does the boat arrive?) but **¿Sabe él cuando llega el buque?** (Does he know when the boat arrives?).

The 'Imitated Pronunciation'

For the first four lessons we give the imitated pronunciation of each new word, in footnotes to the section or vocabulary list in which they first appear. In this imitated pronunciation the Spanish sounds are represented by English syllables; read it as if each syllable were part of an English word and you should always be understood, more especially if you bear in mind the modifications noted below.

When reading the imitated pronunciation, remember that:

th (printed bold face) must be pronounced like 'th' in 'thin', *never* as in 'they'.

H (printed as a capital) is to be pronounced gutturally, like 'ch' in the Scottish 'loch' (*not* 'lock').

s is always like 'ss' in 'missing', *never* like 's' in 'easy'.

ah represents the Spanish a; this sounds like 'ah', but it is shorter than in 'harm', 'cast'. It is *never* like the 'a' in 'hat', but remember to keep it short and sharp.

o resembles the sound of 'o' in 'not', and even slightly approaches the 'aw' in 'law'. It is not as long as in 'go'.

Lesson 1

1 Articles

Articles ('the', 'a', etc) agree in gender and number with the noun to which they relate. Thus, if the noun is masculine and singular, the preceding article must also be masculine singular (indicated by *m.s.* in the paragraphs below, with similar abbreviations for feminine and plural).
The definite article 'the' is expressed by:

el (*m.s*)	**el libro** the book
la (*f.s.*)	**la casa** the house
los (*m.pl.*)	**los libros** the books
las (*f.pl.*)	**las casas** the houses

The indefinite article 'a', 'an', 'some' is expressed by:

un (*m.s.*)	**un libro** a book
una (*f.s.*)	**una casa** a house
unos (*m.pl.*)	**unos libros** (some) books
unas (*f.pl.*)	**unas casas** (some) houses

NOTE: The masculine article is used before a feminine singular noun beginning with **a** or **ha,** if the **a** or **ha** takes the stress:

el agua water
el hambre hunger

IMITATED PRONUNCIATION (1): ell 'lee-bro; lah 'kah-sah; los 'lee-bros; lahs 'kah-sahs; oon 'lee-bro; 'oo-nah 'kah-sah; 'oo-nos 'lee-bros; 'oo-nahs 'kah-sahs; ell 'ah-goo'ah; ell 'ahm-bray.

2 Nouns

All nouns are either masculine or feminine. There are no neuter nouns. Most nouns ending in **o** are masculine. Most nouns ending in **a, ión, d, z** are feminine. There are exceptions however:

11

√ **la mano** (*f.*)   hand
el camión (*m.*)   lorry
el lápiz (*m.*)   pencil
el guardia (*m.*)   policeman   el policía

Several words ending in **a** (of Greek origin) are masculine:

el telegrama   telegram
el idioma   language
el mapa   map

Nouns ending in other letters are of varying genders:

el hombre   man
la mujer   woman
la leche   milk
el color   colour

IMITATED PRONUNCIATION (2): lah 'mah-no; ell kah-me-'on; ell 'lah-pith; ell goo''ah-de-ah; ell tay-lay-'grah-mah; ell e-de-'o-mah; ell 'mah-pah; ell 'om-bray; lah moo-'Hairr; lah 'lay-chay; ell ko-'lorr.

3 Plural of nouns

1) The plural of nouns is formed by adding **s** to nouns ending in a vowel, and **es** to nouns ending in a consonant:

hombre (man→**hombres** (men)
mujer (woman)→**mujeres** (women)

2) The plural of nouns ending in **z** is formed by changing the **z into c** and adding **es**:

lápiz (pencil)→**lápices** (pencils)
luz (light)→**luces** (lights)

3) Nouns ending in a consonant and bearing an accent on the last syllable lose that accent when the plural is formed:

camión (lorry)→**camiones** (lorries)

IMITATED PRONUNCIATION (3): 'om-brace; moo-'Hairr-ace; 'lah-pith-ace; looth; 'looth-ace; kah-me-'on-ace.

Exercise 1

Form the plural of:
1 El libro   (book)
2 La casa   (house)
3 La mujer   (woman)
4 El hombre   (man)
5 La calle   (street)
6 La flor   (flower)
7 El jardín   (garden)
8 El coche   (car)
9 La capital   (capital)
10 La ciudad   (city, town)
11 La luz   (light)
12 La ley   (law)

IMITATED PRONUNCIATION (Ex.1): 5 'kah-l'yay; 6 florr; 7 Harr-'deen; 8 'ko-chay; 9 kah-pe-'tahl; 10 the'oo-'dahd; 12 'lay'e.

Exercise 2

Put the appropriate definite article before the following nouns:
1 ... cigarrillos   (*m.*, cigarettes)
2 ... vino   (*m.*, wine)
3 ... mesas   (*f.*, tables)
✓ 4 ... cerveza   (*f.*, beer)
5 ... pez   (*m.*, fish)
6 ... árboles   (*m.*, trees)
7 ...padre   (*m.*, father)
8 ... madre   (*f.*, mother)
9 ... lápiz   (*m.*, pencil)
10 ... estaciones   (*f.*, stations)
11 ... billete   (*m.*, ticket)
12 ... tren   (*m.*, train)

Repeat the above exercise using the indefinite article

IMITATED PRONUNCIATION (Ex. 2): the-gar-'rree-l'yos; 'vee-no; 'may-sahs; thairr-'vay-thah; peth; 'arr-bol-ace; 'pah-dray; 'mah-dray; 'lah-pith; ess-tah-the-'on-ace; be-l''yay-tay; trren.

Exercise 3

Translate:

1 the book	7 a city
2 the table	8 some cigarettes
3 the tickets	9 the garden
4 some trees	10 a street
5 a beer	11 some women
6 the car	12 the station

4 Subject pronouns

singular

yo	I
tú	you (*fam.*)
él, ella	he, she
usted	you (*pol.*)

plural

nosotros (*m.*), **nosotras** (*f.*)	we
vosotros (*m.*), **vosotras** (*f.*)	you (*fam.*)
ellos (*m.*), **ellas** (*f.*)	they
ustedes	you (*pol.*)

The forms **tú** and **vosotros/as** (familiar forms) are used to address members of the family, friends, children and animals. The forms **usted** and **ustedes** (polite forms) are used to address all other people; usually written as **Vd.** and **Vds.**, they must always be used with the 3rd person of the verb. **Usted** is a contraction of the archaic form of address **Vuestra Merced,** 'your honour'. Although the familiar form is becoming increasingly common in Spain, it is still advisable to use the polite form when addressing strangers or people you have just met.

Except for **usted** and **ustedes** (which are nearly always expressed), all other subject pronouns are omitted unless emphasis is required or ambiguity must be avoided.

IMITATED PRONUNCIATION (4): yo; too; ell; 'ell-yah; oos-'ted; nos-'o-tros; nos-'o-trahs; vos-'o-tros; vos-'o-trahs; 'ell-yos; 'ell-yahs; oos-'tay-dace.

5 Other forms of address

The titles **señor** (Mr.), **señora** (Mrs.) and **señorita** (Miss) are used in front of the person's surname and are always preceded by the definite article except when the person is addressed directly. They are usually written as: **Sr., Sra., Srta.**

El Sr. Martínez.   Mr. Martínez.
La Sra. Martínez.   Mrs. Martínez.
La Srta. Martínez.   Miss Martínez.
Por aquí, Sr. Martínez.   This way, Mr. Martínez.

The titles **Don** and **Doña,** for which there is no equivalent in English, are used in front of the person's Christian name. Thus:

Don Juan; Doña María

IMITATED PRONUNCIATION (5): say-n''yorr; say-n''yor-rah; say-n'yor-'ree-tah; marr-'tee-neth; porr ah-'kee; don Hoo''ahn; 'don-yah mah-'rree-ah.

6 The verb 'tener' (to have, to possess)

This is an irregular verb, and one of the most important in the language, so learn it thoroughly.

Present tense

tengo	I have
tienes	you have
tiene	he, she has, you have (*polite form*)
tenemos	we have
tenéis	you have
tienen	they have, you have (*polite form*)

Tienen una hija.   They have a daughter.
Tenemos un coche.   We have a car.

IMITATED PRONUNCIATION (6): tay-'nairr; 'ten-go; te-'ay-nace; te-'ay-nay; tay-'nay-mos; tay-'nay-iss; te-'ay-nen; 'ee-Hah.

7 Negative form

The negative is formed by putting the word **no** in front of the verb:

No tengo dinero.   I have no money.
No tienen cerveza.   They haven't (any) beer.

8 Interrogative form

A sentence is made interrogative by putting the subject after the
verb:
Vd. tiene una pluma.   You have a pen.
¿Tiene Vd. una pluma?   Have you a pen?

The interrogative is also indicated by intonation in the voice and the
use of an inverted question mark at the beginning of a written
question.

9 Idiomatic uses of 'tener'

There are a number of idioms with **tener** followed by a noun, where
English has 'to be' followed by an adjective. Here are some
examples:

tener calor	to be hot
tener cuidado	to be careful
tener éxito	to be successful
tener frío	to be cold
tener hambre	to be hungry
tener miedo	to be afraid
tener razón	to be right
tener sed	to be thirsty
tener sueño	to be sleepy
tener suerte	to be lucky

When **tener que** is followed by an infinitive, it translates 'to have to',
'must':

Tengo que salir.   I have to go out.
Tenemos que ver la iglesia.   We must see the church.

IMITATED PRONUNCIATION (9): kah-'lor; koo'e-'dah-do; 'ex-e-to;
'frree-o; 'ahm-bray; mee-'ay-do; rrah-'thon; sayd; soo''ay-n'yo;
soo''air-tay; tay-'nairr kay; sah-'leerr; vairr; e-'glay-se-ah.

As you work through the lessons, your vocabulary will steadily be increased by the introduction of new words in the sentences that illustrate grammar explanations. Additional vocabulary lists like the one below, where fresh words are shown in the order you will come upon them in the following exercise, should be learnt before you begin the written translation work. If you find a word repeated, and you've learnt it already, don't worry!

Vocabulary

el café	coffee
trabajar	to work
todo	everything
salir	to go out
el hijo	son

IMITATED PRONUNCIATION: kah-'fay; trah-bah-'Harr; 'to-do; sah-'leerr; 'ee-Ho.

Exercise 4

Translate:
1 They have a house.
2 We haven't (any) coffee.
3 The man is afraid.
4 I have to work.
5 Have you (*fam. sing.*) a pencil?
6 They are not thirsty.
7 Have you (*pol. pl.*) everything?
8 I am hot.
9 We have to go out.
10 He has a son.

Drill

In this and similar drills that follow, first read the example which shows both a 'stimulus' and a 'response' (not necessarily a simple question and answer). The model will show you how to tackle the rest of that drill. Thus, in the following you will see that the stimulus requires a response alternating between the first persons singular and plural.

18

1 ¿Tiene Vd. una pluma?	Have you a pen?
No, no tengo una pluma.	No, I haven't a pen.
¿Tienen Vds. un lápiz?	Have you (*pl.*) a pencil?
No, no tenemos un lápiz.	No, we haven't a pencil.

1 ¿Tiene Vd. hambre?
2 ¿Tienen Vds. cerveza?
3 ¿Tiene Vd. sed?
4 ¿Tienen Vds. calor?
5 ¿Tiene Vd. frío?
6 ¿Tienen Vds. los libros?
7 ¿Tiene Vd. cigarrillos?
8 ¿Tienen Vds. los billetes?

CONVERSATIONS

a)

Sr. **¿Tiene Vd. una cerveza muy fría? Tengo sed.** Have you a very cold beer? I am thirsty.

Sra. **Sí, señor. Aquí tiene.** Yes, Sir. Here you are.

Sr. **¿Cuánto es?** How much is it?

Sra. **Cincuenta pesetas.** Fifty pesetas.

Sr. **Sólo tengo un billete de mil. ¿Tiene Vd. cambio?** I only have a one thousand peseta note. Have you got change?

Sra. **Sí, señor.** Yes, sir.

Sr. **Gracias. Adiós.** Thank you. Goodbye.

b)

Sra. **Carmen y Luis tienen un piso en la ciudad y una casa en el campo.** Carmen and Luis have a flat in town and a house in the country.

Sr. **¿Tiene la casa un jardín grande?** Has the house got a large garden?

Sra. **Sí, muy grande y muy bonito, con árboles y flores. También tienen un perro y un gato.** Yes, very big and very pretty, with trees and flowers. They also have a dog and a cat.

Lesson 2

10 Contraction of article

When the prepositions **a** (to) and **de** (of, from) are followed by the definite article **el** they contract into **al** and **del** respectively:

al castillo   to the castle
del jardín   from the garden

11 Possession

There is no possessive case in Spanish. Possession must be expressed by the preposition **de**:

El padre de Juan.   John's father (*lit.* The father of John).
El paraguas de la mujer.   The woman's umbrella.

IMITATED PRONUNCIATION (10/11): ah, day; ahl kahs-'teel-l'yo; dayl Harr-'deen; 'pah-dray; pah-'rrah-goo'ahs.

Exercise 5

Translate:
 1 to the church.
 2 of the language.
 3 to the car.
 4 to the table.
 5 of the trees.
 6 to the house.
 7 of the man.
 8 of the city.
 9 to the street.
10 of the wine.
11 to the policeman.
12 of the station.

12 Adjectives

✓ Adjectives <u>agree in gender and number</u> with the nouns they qualify and generally <u>follow the noun</u>. Adjectives ending in **o** in the masculine change the **o** to **a** in the feminine. The plural is formed by adding **s** to both genders:

El coche blanco.   The white car.
La casa blanca.   The white house.
Los coches blancos.   The white cars.
Las casas blancas.   The white houses.

✓ Adjectives ending in **e**, and most adjectives ending in a consonant, have the <u>same form for both masculine and feminine</u>. The plural is formed by adding **s** to those ending in **e**, and **es** to those ending in a consonant. For example:

El lápiz verde.   The green pencil.
La pared verde.   The green wall.
Los lápices verdes.   The green pencils.
Las paredes verdes.   The green walls.
Un ejercicio fácil.   An easy exercise.
Una lección fácil.   An easy lesson.
Unos ejercicios fáciles.   Some easy exercises.
Unas lecciones fáciles.   Some easy lessons.

Exceptions to this rule are:

a) adjectives of nationality

inglés   English (*m.*)
inglesa   English (*f.*)
español   Spanish (*m.*)
española   Spanish (*f.*)

b) certain adjectives ending in **n** and **or**

holgazán   lazy (*m.*)
holgazana   lazy (*f.*)
trabajador   hard-working (*m.*)
trabajadora   hard-working (*f.*)

IMITATED PRONUNCIATION (12): 'blahn-ko; 'blahn-kah; 'blahn-kos; 'blahn-kahs; 'vairr-day; pah-'reth; 'vairr-dace; pah-'reth-ace; ay-Hairr-'thee-the-o; 'fah-thil; leck-the-'on; ay-Hairr-'thee-the-os;

'fah-**th**il-ace; leck-**the**-'on-ace; in-'gless; in-'gless-ah; es-pah-'n'yol; es-pah'n'yo-lah; ol-gah-'**th**ahn; ol-gah-'**th**ahn-ah; trah-bah-Hah-'dorr; trah-bah-Hah-'dor-rah.

Vocabulary

el periódico	newspaper
la revista	magazine
interesante	interesting
encantador	charming
bueno	good
útil	useful
barato	cheap
largo	long
alto	tall
alemán / alemána	German

IMITATED PRONUNCIATION: pay-rre-'o-de-ko; rray-'viss-tah; in-tay-ress-'an-tay; en-kahn-tah-'dorr; boo''ay-no; 'oo-til; bah-'rah-to; 'lar-go; 'ahl-to; ah-lay-'mahn.

Exercise 6

Make the following adjectives agree where necessary:
1 Unos hombres bueno.
2 Una mujer encantador.
3 Unos libros útil.
4 Unas flores blanco.
5 Un coche barato.
6 Una calle largo.
7 Unos árboles alto.
8 Unas ciudades interesante.
9 Un periódico inglés.
10 Una revista alemán.

13 'Ser' and 'estar'

It is important to distinguish between the verbs **ser** and **estar**, both of which translate the English 'to be'.

22

Present tenses

ser	estar	
soy	estoy	I am
eres	estás	you are
es	está	he/she is, you are (*pol.*)
somos	estamos	we are
sois	estáis	you are
son	están	they are, you are (*pol.*)

IMITATED PRONUNCIATION (13): sairr; es-'tahrr; soy; 'eh-ress; ess; 'so-mos; 'so' ees; son; es-'toy; es-'tahs; es-'tah; es-'tah-mos; es-'tah'ees; es-'tahn.

14 Uses of 'ser'

Ser expresses an inherent characteristic or permanent state and it is used to indicate:

a) Identity
   Soy Carmen.   I am Carmen.

b) Possession
   El perro es de Juan.   The dog is John's.

c) Origin
   Mis amigos son de Madrid.   My friends are from Madrid.

d) Nationality
   Somos ingleses.   We are English.

e) Occupation
   El padre de María es arquitecto.   Maria's father is an architect.

f) Material of which something is made
   El reloj es de oro.   The watch is made of gold.

g) Inherent characteristics
   Carlos es muy alto.   Charles is very tall.

h) Expressions of time
   Son las cinco.   It is five o'clock.
   Hoy es lunes.   Today is Monday.

i) Impersonal expressions
   Es mejor esperar. It is better to wait.
   Es difícil aprender. It is difficult to learn.

Ser is also used with the past participle of the verb to form the
passive voice (see page 97 for further notes on the passive):

El ladrón es apresado por la policía. The thief is captured by the
police.

IMITATED PRONUNCIATION (14): 'pairr-o; mees ah-'mee-gos;
mah-'dreeth; arr-ke-'tect-o; rray-'loH; 'o-ro; moo'e; 'thin-ko; oy'e;
'loo-ness; may-'Horr; ess-pay-'rahrr; de-'fee-thil; ah-pren-'dairr;
lah-'dron; ah-pray-'sah-do; po-le-'thee-ah.

15 Uses of 'estar'

Estar is used to indicate:

a) Temporary states or conditions
    Pedro está enfermo. Peter is ill.

b) Position (whether temporary or permanent)
    Carmen está en el salón. Carmen is in the lounge.
    Valencia está en España. Valencia is in Spain.

Estar is also used with the present participle of the verb to form the
continuous tenses:

Los niños están jugando en el jardín. The children are playing in
the garden.

Estar with the preposition **para** translates 'to be about to':

El tren está para llegar. The train is about to arrive.

These basic rules, however, do not cover every situation. There are
cases where it is difficult for the student to decide which verb is the
right one. For instance, it can be argued that to be young (**joven**) or
to be rich (**rico**) is a temporary condition, but in both cases **ser** is
used. In the following exercise an English translation will help you
decide whether each sentence is 'temporary' or 'permanent'.

IMITATED PRONUNCIATION (15): en-'fairr-mo; sah-'lonn;
vah-'len-the-ah; ess-'pah-n'yah; 'nee-n'yos; Hoo-'gahn-do;
'pah-rrah; l'yay-'garr; 'Ho-ven; 'rree-ko.

Exercise 7

Write down these sentences in Spanish, with the appropriate form of 'ser' or 'estar' where we have omitted them.

1	Las lecciones ...... difíciles.	The lessons are difficult.
2	El café ...... frío.	The coffee is cold.
3	Las chicas ...... alemanas.	The girls are German.
4	Jaime ...... muy inteligente.	James is very intelligent.
5	Los libros ...... sobre la mesa.	The books are on the table.
6	Ana ...... triste.	Ann is sad.
7	La mujer de Luis ...... secretaria.	Luis's wife is a secretary.
8	La casa ...... pequeña.	The house is small.
9	El coche no ...... en el garaje.	The car is not in the garage.
10	Yo ...... contento con el hotel.	I am pleased with the hotel.

IMITATED PRONUNCIATION (Ex. 7): 'chee-kahs; 'so-bray; 'triss-tay; say-kray-'tah-ree-ah; pay-'kay-n'yah; gah-'rrah-Hay; con-'ten-to; con.

Vocabulary

italiano	Italian
la manzana	apple
en	in
la cocina	kitchen
el autobús	bus
allí	there
la capital	capital
España	Spain
la colina	hill
peligroso	dangerous
fumar	to smoke
demasiado	too much
dulce	sweet
mañana	tomorrow
domingo	Sunday
la playa	beach

IMITATED PRONUNCIATION: ee-tah-lee-'ah-no; mahn-'thah-nah; en; ko-'thee-nah; ah'oo-to-'booss; ah-'l'yee; kah-pe-'tahl; ess-'pahn-yah; ko-'lee-nah; pay-le-'gro-so; foo-'mahr; day-mah-se-'ah-do; 'dool-thay; mah-'n'yah-nah; do-'meen-go; 'plah-yah.

Exercise 8

Translate:
1 She is Italian.
2 The apples are in the kitchen.
3 The bus is over there.
4 Madrid is the capital of Spain.
5 The girl is tall.
6 The house is on the hill.
7 It is dangerous to smoke.
8 The coffee is too sweet.
9 Tomorrow is Sunday.
10 They are on the beach.

CONVERSATIONS

a)

Juan	**¿Dónde está tu padre?** Where is your father?
Teresa	**Está en el jardín, tomando el sol y leyendo el periódico.** He is in the garden sunbathing and reading the paper.
Juan	**Y tu madre ¿dónde está?** And your mother, where is she?
Teresa	**Está en la cocina haciendo una paella para la comida.** She is in the kitchen making a 'paella' for lunch.
Juan	**¡Una paella! ¡Qué bien!** 'Paella'! How lovely!

b)

Recepcionista	**¿Es Vd. el señor García?** Are you Mr. Garcia?
Sr. García	**Sí.** Yes.
Recepcionista	**Tengo un telegrama para Vd.** I have a telegram for you.
Sr. García	**¿De dónde es el telegrama?** Where is the telegram from?
Recepcionista	**Es de Londres.** It's from London.
Sr. García	**Ah! Muchas gracias.** Oh! Thank you.
Recepcionista	**De nada.** Not at all.

Lesson 3

16 Demonstrative adjectives

	Masculine	*Feminine*
this	este	esta
that	ese	esa
that (over there)	aquel	aquella
these	estos	estas
those	esos	esas
those (over there)	aquellos	aquellas

Demonstrative adjectives always precede the noun and agree with it in gender and number:

Este coche.   This car.
Esa iglesia.   That church.
Aquellos niños.   Those children (over there).

Vocabulary

caro	expensive
fuerte	strong
muy	very
viejo	old
el amigo	friend
ocupado	occupied, taken, busy
libre	free
el ascensor	lift
lleno	full
la uva	grape
agrio	sour

IMITATED PRONUNCIATION (16/Vocab): 'es-tay; 'ay-say; ah-'kel; 'es-tos; 'ay-sos; ah-'kell-yos; 'es-tah; 'ay-sah; ah-'kell-yah; 'es-tahs; 'ay-sahs; ah-'kell-yahs; 'kah-ro; foo''air-tay; 'moo'e; ve-'ay-Ho; ah-'mee-go; o-koo-'pah-do; 'lee-bray; ahs-**then**-'sor; 'l'yay-no; 'oo-vah; 'ah-gre-o.

Exercise 9

Translate:
1 That car is expensive.
2 Those cigarettes are strong.
3 That church is very old.
4 These friends are from Malaga.
5 This table is taken.
6 That man is free.
7 This lift is full.
8 Those grapes are sour.
9 Those books (over there) are interesting.
10 It is that beach (over there).

17 Demonstrative pronouns

These have the same forms as the adjectives but take an accent on the stressed syllable. They agree in gender and number with the noun they replace. For example:

No es este libro, es aquél.   It isn't this book, it's that one over there.
Estos zapatos son caros, ésos son baratos.   These shoes are expensive, those are cheap.

The neuter forms of the pronoun **esto** (this) and **eso, aquello** (that) are used to refer to things the gender of which has not been established. These forms have no plural.

¿Qué es esto?   What is this?
Eso no es correcto.   That is not correct.

Vocabulary

la maleta	suitcase
la galleta	biscuit
el pan	bread
el abrigo	coat
el zapato	shoe
el vino	wine
la habitación	room

IMITATED PRONUNCIATION: mah-'lay-tah; gahl-'yay-tah; pahn; ah-'bree-go; **thah**-'pah-to; 'vee-no; ah-be-tah-**the**-'on.

Exercise 10

Replace the words in brackets by the correct form of the demonstrative adjective or pronoun:

1 No son (these) libros, son (those ones).
2 No es (that) maleta, es (that one over there).
3 No son (these) galletas, son (those ones).
4 No es (that) pan, es (this one).
5 No es (this) abrigo, es (that one over there).
6 No son (those) zapatos, son (these ones).
7 No es (this) vino, es (that one).
8 No es (that) periódico, es (this one).
9 No son (these) habitaciones, son (those ones).
10 No es (this) coche, es (that one over there).

18 Regular verbs

The infinitive of every Spanish verb ends in **ar, er** or **ir** (hab**lar**, com**er**, viv**ir**). The part preceding these endings is called the stem. Most tenses are formed by adding certain personal endings to the stem. These endings are shown in bold letters, below:

Present tenses

hablar (to speak)	**comer** (to eat)	**vivir** (to live)
habl**o**	com**o**	viv**o**
habl**as**	com**es**	viv**es**
habl**a**	com**e**	viv**e**
habl**amos**	com**emos**	viv**imos**
habl**áis**	com**éis**	viv**ís**
habl**an**	com**en**	viv**en**

No hablo ruso. I don't speak Russian.
¿Habla Vd. español? Do you speak Spanish?
Come mucho pan. He eats a lot of bread.
No comen en el hotel. They don't eat in the hotel.
¿Viven Vds. aquí? Do you live here?
Vivo en Londres. I live in London.

Vocabulary

comprar	to buy
beber	to drink
escribir	to write
fumar	to smoke
estudiar	to study
aprender	to learn
subir	to go up, to bring up

IMITATED PRONUNCIATION (18/Vocab): ah-'blahrr; 'ah-blo; 'ah-blahs; 'ah-blah; ah-'blah-mos; ah-'blah-ees; 'ah-blahn; ko-'mairr; 'ko-mo; 'ko-mes; 'ko-may; ko-'may-mos; ko-'may-ees; 'ko-men; ve-'veer; 'vee-vo; 'vee-ves; 'vee-vay; ve-'vee-mos; ve-'vees; 'vee-ven; 'rroo-so; 'moo-cho; 'lon-dress; kom-'prahrr; bay-'bair; ess-kre-'beerr; foo-'mahrr; ess-too-de-'ahrr; ah-pren-'dairr; soo-'beerr.

In listening to the recording of vivir in particular, students will have noticed the tendency towards pronouncing 'v' as 'b'. This is what you'll hear more often than not in Spain, and – as we point out in the introductory paragraph dealing with varying pronunciations – it is quite acceptable and not incorrect. However, throughout the printed text we have imitated the Spanish 'v' with an English 'v'.

Exercise 11

Translate:
1 I buy.
2 He smokes.
3 You (*pol. s.*) drink.
4 We write.
5 They learn.
6 I study.
7 You (*fam. s.*) speak.
8 She eats.
9 We live.
10 They go up.
11 I learn.
12 He drinks.

Exercise 12

Translate:
1 He buys a newspaper.
2 Does she drink beer?
3 Pedro lives in Barcelona.
4 I write to Conchita.
5 Do you study English?
6 These children learn Spanish.
7 He eats too much.
8 We go up the hill.
9 I speak English.
10 They smoke cheap cigarettes.

19 Present participle

The present participle of regular verbs is formed by adding -**ando** to the stem of verbs in **ar,** and -**iendo** to the stem of verbs in **er** and **ir.** For example:

hablar→**hablando** (speaking)
comer→**comiendo** (eating)
vivir→**viviendo** (living)

The present participle used with the present tense of the verb **estar** forms the present continuous tenses ('I am speaking', 'I am eating', 'I am living' etc):

Present continuous

hablar	**comer**	**vivir**
estoy hablando	estoy comiendo	estoy viviendo
estás hablando	estás comiendo	estás viviendo
está hablando	está comiendo	está viviendo
estamos hablando	estamos comiendo	estamos viviendo
estáis hablando	estáis comiendo	estáis viviendo
están hablando	están comiendo	están viviendo

Ramón está bebiendo vino.   Ramón is drinking wine.
El gato está subiendo al árbol.   The cat is going up the tree.
Estoy aprendiendo francés.   I am learning French.

These tenses have a more restricted use in Spanish than in English.

They generally indicate an action taking place at the time of speaking.

IMITATED PRONUNCIATION (19): ah-'blahn-do; ko-me-'en-do; vee-ve-'en-do; rrah-'mon; bay-be-'en-do; 'gah-to; soo-be-'en-do; ah-pren-de-'en-do; frahn-'thess.

20 Interrogative pronouns

¿Qué? What?
¿Quién? ¿Quiénes?(*pl.*) Who? Whom?
¿De quién? Whose?
¿Cuál? ¿Cuáles?(*pl.*) Which? What?

¿Qué come Vd.? What do you eat?
¿Quién es Vd.? Who are you?
¿De quién es esta pluma? Whose is this pen?

¿Cuál de estos trenes va a Valencia? Which of these trains goes to Valencia?
¿Cuál es su nombre? What is your name?

¿Qué? can sometimes play the role of an adjective:
¿Qué libros desea Vd.? Which books do you want?

21 Relative pronouns

(a) **que** who, which, that
La chica que cuida a los niños. The girl who looks after the children.
El coche que conduce. The car he drives.

(b) **quien, quienes** whom.
Used generally after prepositions:
El profesor con quien estudio. The teacher with whom I study.
El hombre para quien trabaja. The man for whom he works.

(c) The forms **el que, la que, los que, las que** and **el cual, la cual, los cuales, las cuales** can refer to persons or things and they translate 'whom' or 'which' after a preposition:
La mujer con la que está hablando. The woman with whom he is speaking.

El autobús en el que viajo. The bus in which I travel.
Los amigos a los cuales escribo. The friends to whom I write.

(d) 'who' is translated by **quien, quienes** after part of the verb 'to be' and a noun or pronoun.
Es él quien tiene la culpa. It is he who is to blame.
Es María quien tiene que escribir. It is María who has to write.

(e) **cuyo(-a,-os,-as)** whose, of whom, of which.
This is a relative adjective and it agrees in gender and number with the following noun.
El hombre cuya hija es actriz. The man whose daughter is an actress.

(f) **Lo que** what
In this context, 'what' refers to a clause or an idea:
No comprendo lo que dice. I don't understand what he says.
No sabe lo que comprar. He doesn't know what to buy.

Note that the relative pronoun can never be omitted in Spanish:
El hombre *que* **deseo ver.** The man I want to see.
El libro *que* **lee.** The book he reads.

IMITATED PRONUNCIATION (20/21): kay; ke-'en; ke-'en-ess; koo''ahl; koo''ahl-ess; koo''ee-dah; kon-'doo-thay; pro-fay-'sorr; ve''ah-Ho; ess-'kree-bo; 'kool-pah; 'koo-yo; 'koo-yah; 'koo-yoss; 'koo-yahss; ac-'treeth; lo kay; 'dee-thay; 'sah-bay; day-'say-o; vairr; lay'ee.

Vocabulary

el pueblo	village
la tienda	shop
leer (leyendo)	to read (reading)
el médico	doctor
la carta	letter
verde	green
la puerta	door
la pluma	pen
con	with
el número	number

IMITATED PRONUNCIATION: poo''ay-blo; te-'en-dah; lay-'airr; lay-'en-do; 'may-de-ko; 'kahrr-tah; 'vairr-day; poo''air-tah; 'ploo-mah; kon; 'noo-may-ro.

Exercise 13

Translate:
1 The village in which we live.
2 The woman who works in the shop.
3 The book that I have to read.
4 The town of which we are speaking.
5 It is Pedro who is (a) doctor.
6 Whose letters are these?
7 Which magazine is he buying?
8 The house which has a green door.
9 The pen with which I write.
10 What is the number?

Drills

2 ¿Son Vds. ingleses?   Are you (*pl.*) English?
Sí, somos ingleses.   Yes, we're English.

¿Es Vd. inglés?   Are you English?
Sí, soy inglés.   Yes, I'm English.

1 ¿Beben Vds. cerveza?
2 ¿Come Vd. pan?
3 ¿Viven Vds. en Londres?
4 ¿Es Vd. médico?
5 ¿Hablan Vds. español?
6 ¿Compra Vd. la revista?

3 ¿Es Vd. inglés?   Are you English?
No, no soy inglés.   No, I'm not English.

¿Son Vds. ingleses?   Are you (*pl.*) English?
No, no somos ingleses.   No, we're not English.

1 ¿Vive Vd. en Barcelona?
2 ¿Fuman Vds.?
3 ¿Aprende Vd. alemán?
4 ¿Compran Vds. los periódicos?
5 ¿Bebe Vd. vino?
6 ¿Son Vds. españoles?

4 *Replace the blanks by the correct form of the present continuous:*
¿Qué come? Está comiendo pan.

1 ¿Qué compra? ...... el periódico.
2 ¿Qué beben? ...... cerveza.
3 ¿Qué estudia Vd.? ...... español.
4 ¿Qué comen Vds.? ...... uvas.
5 ¿Qué lee? ...... una revista.
6 ¿Qué fuma Vd.? ...... un cigarrillo.
7 ¿Qué hablan Vds.? ...... inglés.
8 ¿Qué escribe? ...... una carta.
9 ¿Qué aprenden? ...... español.
10 ¿Qué sube Vd.? ...... las maletas.

CONVERSATION

En la librería
At the bookshop

Dependienta **¿Buenos días, señor. ¿Qué desea?** Good morning, Sir. Can I help you?

Cliente **Buenos días. ¿Tiene Vd. un libro de historia de España?** Good morning. Have you a book on the history of Spain?

Dependienta **Sí, señor, tenemos varios. Este es muy bueno, tiene muchas ilustraciones.** Yes, Sir, we have several. This one is very good, it has many illustrations.

Cliente **Sí, parece muy interesante. ¿Cuánto es?** Yes, it looks very interesting. How much is it?

Dependienta **Ochocientas pesetas.** Eight hundred pesetas.

Cliente **Es un poco caro. Y ése ¿cuánto es?** It is a little expensive. And that one, how much is it?

Dependienta **Ese, quinientas.** That one, five hundred.

Cliente **Muy bien, ése por favor.** All right, that one please.

Lesson 4

22 Possessive adjectives

	singular	plural
my	**mi**	**mis**
your	**tu**	**tus**
his, her, its, your (*pol.*)	**su**	**sus**
our	**nuestro (-a)**	**nuestros (-as)**
your	**vuestro (-a)**	**vuestros (-as)**
their, your (*pol.*)	**su**	**sus**

Possessive adjectives agree with the thing possessed, not with the possessor:

Mi coche.   My car.
Mis hermanos.   My brothers.
Nuestro perro.   Our dog.
Nuestras hijas.   Our daughters.

Although, 'his', 'her', 'its', 'their' and 'your' are all translated by the forms **su** and **sus,** the meaning is usually clear from the context. However, in cases of ambiguity the following forms can be used: **de él, de ella, de ellos, de ellas, de Vd., de Vds.:**

El libro de Vd.   Your book.
El amigo de ellos.   Their friend.

Vocabulary

el hermano	brother
la hermana	sister
el tío	uncle
la tía	aunt
el marido	husband
la mujer	wife
el primo	cousin
la prima	cousin (*f.*)

35

el sobrino	nephew
el sobrina	niece
los padres	parents
los parientes	relatives

IMITATED PRONUNCIATION (22/Vocab): me; mees; too; toos; soo; sooss, etc; airr-'mahn-o; airr-'mahn-ah; 'tee-o; 'tee-ah; mah-'ree-do; moo-'Hairr; 'pree-mo; 'pree-mah; so-'bree-no; so-'bree-nah; 'pah-drace; pah-re-'en-tace.

Exercise 14

Translate:
1 My husband.
2 Her brother.
3 Our sister.
4 Their nephew.
5 His uncle.
6 My parents.
7 Your wife.
8 Their sons.
9 Your (*pol.s.*) cousin (*m.*).
10 His relatives.

23 Possessive pronouns

	singular	*plural*
mine	el mío, la mía	los míos, las mías
yours	el tuyo, la tuya	los tuyos, las tuyas
his, hers, its, yours (*pol.*)	el suyo, la suya	los suyos, las suyas
ours	el nuestro, la nuestra	los nuestros, las nuestras
yours	el vuestro, la vuestra	los vuestros, las vuestras
theirs, yours (*pol.*)	el suyo, la suya	los suyos, las suyas

Possessive pronouns agree in gender and number with the noun they replace. They are always preceded by the definite article, except after the verb **ser** when the article is usually omitted. For example:
Mi casa y la tuya.   My house and yours.
Estas cartas son nuestras.   These letters are ours.

These forms are also used as adjectives, after the noun and without the article, to translate 'of mine', 'of yours', etc:

Un amigo mío. A friend of mine.
Una idea suya. An idea of his.

IMITATED PRONUNCIATION (23): 'me'o; 'me'ah; 'me-os; 'me-ahs; 'too-yo, etc; 'soo-yo, etc.

Exercise 15

Replace the word in brackets by the appropriate form of the possessive pronoun:
1 Mi casa y (yours, *fam.s.*)
2 Nuestro jardín y (theirs).
3 Su coche y (ours).
4 Mi mujer y (his).
5 Vuestra madre y (ours).
6 Su padre y (mine).
7 Mi cerveza y (yours, *pol.*).
8 Nuestros amigos y (yours, *fam.pl.*).
9 Su secretaria y (mine).
10 Tu gato y (hers).

24 Cardinal numbers

1	uno (*m.*), una (*f.*)	14	catorce
2	dos	15	quince
3	tres	16	dieciséis
4	cuatro	17	diecisiete
5	cinco	18	dieciocho
6	seis	19	diecinueve
7	siete	20	veinte
8	ocho	21	veintiuno (-a)
9	nueve	22	veintidós
10	diez	23	veintitrés, etc
11	once	30	treinta
12	doce	31	treinta y uno (-a)
13	trece	32	treinta y dos

40	cuarenta	700	setecientos (-as)
50	cincuenta	800	ochocientos (-as)
60	sesenta	900	novecientos (-as)
70	setenta	1,000	mil
80	ochenta	1,001	mil uno (-a)
90	noventa	1,002	mil dos
100	cien, ciento	1,100	mil cien
101	ciento uno (-a)	1,101	mil ciento uno (-a)
102	ciento dos	1,200	mil doscientos (-as)
200	doscientos (-as)	2,000	dos mil
300	trescientos (-as)	100,000	cien mil
400	cuatrocientos (-as)	200,000	doscientos mil
500	quinientos (-as)	1,000,000	un millón
600	seiscientos (-as)	2,000,000	dos millones

Uno and **ciento** are contracted to **un** and **cien** in front of a noun or an adjective:

un libro   one book
cien libros   a hundred books

IMITATED PRONUNCIATION: 'oo-no; 'oo-nah; doss; tress; koo''ahr-tro; 'thin-ko; 'say-iss; se-'ay-tay; 'o-cho; noo''ay-vay; de-'eth; 'on-thay; 'do-thay; 'tray-thay; kah-'torr-thay; 'kin-thay; de-'eth-e-'say-iss, etc; (20) 'vay'n-tay; 'vay'n-te-'oo-no, etc; (30) 'tray-in-tah, etc; (40) koo'ah-'ren-tah; thin-koo''en-tah; say-'sen-tah; say-'ten-tah; o-'chen-tah; no-'ven-tah; the-'en; the-'en-to, etc; (1000) meel; (1,000,000) mee-'l'yon.

Exercise 16

Translate:
1 Ten houses.
2 Seventy two pesetas.
3 Two hundred cigarettes.
4 Sixteen letters.
5 One hundred and thirty five books.
6 Forty six hotels.
7 Three hundred and fifty four apples.
8 Sixty eight shops.
9 One thousand four hundred men.
10 Seven hundred and eighty five cars.

25 Ordinal numbers

1st **primero**	6th **sexto**
2nd **segundo**	7th **séptimo**
3rd **tercero**	8th **octavo**
4th **cuarto**	9th **noveno**
5th **quinto**	10th **décimo**

Beyond the 'tenth', cardinal numbers are generally used:

Felipe II (segundo).   Philip II.
Alfonso XII (doce).   Alfonso XII.
El siglo III (tercero).   The third century.
El siglo XX (veinte).   The twentieth century.
El octavo piso.   The eighth floor.
El piso trece.   The thirteenth floor.

Note that with titles and centuries both ordinal and cardinal numbers follow the noun.

All the ordinal numbers form their feminine and plural in the usual way:

La tercera vez.   The third time.
Los primeros días.   The first days.

Primero and **tercero** are shortened to **primer** and **tercer** in front of the masculine noun:

El primer hombre.   The first man.
El tercer niño.   The third child.

IMITATED PRONUNCIATION (25): pre-'may-ro; say-'goon-do; tairr-'thay-ro; koo''ar-to; 'keen-to; 'sex-to; 'sep-te-mo; ock-'tah-vo; no-'vay-no; 'day-**th**e-mo; fay-'lee-pay; ahl-'fon-so; 'see-glo; 'pee-so; ve**th**; 'dee-ahss; pree-'mair; tairr-'**th**airr.

Exercise 17

Translate:
1 The seventh book.
2 The first wife.
3 The third daughter.

4 The sixth cigarette.
5 The second door.
6 The tenth day.
7 The fourth street.
8 The ninth child.
9 The fifth man.
10 The eighth shop.

26 The time

Telling the time is quite easy, as the following examples show:

¿Qué hora es? What is the time?
Es la una. It is one o'clock.
Son las dos. It is two o'clock.
Son las tres. It is three o'clock.

Notice that the feminine article is used because it stands for the unsaid **hora,** and the plural form (in verb as well as article) applies in all hours except one.

'Quarter to' is expressed by **menos cuarto,** 'quarter past' by **y cuarto,** and 'half past' by **y media.** For example:

Son las siete y diez. It is ten past seven.
Es la una menos veinte. It is twenty to one.
Son las ocho y media. It is half past eight.
Son las cinco menos cuarto. It is quarter to five.
Son las nueve y cuarto. It is quarter past nine.

Mediodía is 'midday' and **medianoche** is 'midnight'. If you want to be exact, **a las once en punto** means 'at eleven o'clock precisely'.

'a.m.' is expressed by **de la mañana,** and 'p.m.' by **de la tarde** or **de la noche** (use the latter for the times after 8.30 p.m.). For example:

El tren sale a las nueve de la mañana. The train leaves at 9 a.m.
En España comemos a las tres de la tarde. In Spain we have lunch at 3 p.m.
Pedro llega a su casa a las once de la noche. Peter arrives at his house at 11 p.m.

The expressions **por la mañana** ('in the morning'), **por la tarde** ('in the afternoon', 'in the evening') and **por la noche** ('at night') are used when the time of day is not given:

Ramón trabaja por la mañana. Ramon works in the morning.
Leo en el jardín por la tarde. I read in the garden in the afternoon.
Por la noche todo está en silencio. At night everything is silent.

27 Days of the week

Los días de la semana son:

lunes	Monday
martes	Tuesday
miércoles	Wednesday
jueves	Thursday
viernes	Friday
sábado	Saturday
domingo	Sunday

28 Months of the year

Los meses del año son:

enero	January
febrero	February
marzo	March
abril	April
mayo	May
junio	June
julio	July
agosto	August
septiembre	September
octubre	October
noviembre	November
diciembre	December

42

29 Seasons of the year

Las estaciones del año son:
la primavera   Spring
el verano   Summer
el otoño   Autumn
el invierno   Winter

Note that days, months and seasons are all spelled with a small initial letter, not with a capital as in English.

IMITATED PRONUNCIATION (27/28/29): 'loo-ness; 'mar-tess; me-'air-co-less; Hoo-'ay-vess; ve-'air-ness; 'sah-bah-do; do-'min-go; ay-'nay-ro; fay-'bray-ro; 'mar-tho; ah-'bril; 'mah-yo; 'Hoo-ne-o; 'Hoo-le-o; ah-'gos-to; sep-te-'em-bray; ok-'too-bray; no-ve-'em-bray; dee-the-'em-bray; pre-mah-'vay-rah; vay-'rah-no; o-'to-n'yo; in-ve-'air-no.

30 Dates

The date can be expressed in two different ways:

a) with the verb **estar**
¿A cuántos estamos?   What is the date?

b) with the verb **ser**
¿Qué fecha es hoy?   What is the date today?
Estamos a siete *or* **Es el siete.**   It's the seventh.

The ordinal number is used for the first of the month, the cardinal numbers for the rest:

El primero de mayo.   The first of May.
El quince de octubre.   The fifteenth of October
[Nació] el cuatro de abril de mil novecientos dos.   [He was born on] the 4th April 1902.

Vocabulary

hasta   until
frío   cold

las vacaciones	holidays
el cumpleaños	birthday
generalmente	usually
ir	to go
cenar	to have dinner
el reloj	watch, clock

IMITATED PRONUNCIATION (30/Vocab): 'fay-chah; nah-**th**e-'o; 'ahs-tah; 'free-o; vah-kah-**th**e-'o-ness; koom-play-'ah- n'yos; Hay-nay-rahl-'men-tay; eer; **th**ay-'narr; rray-'loH.

Exercise 18

Translate:

1 What is the time?
2 It is twenty past ten on my watch.
3 I work until half past eleven.
4 The winter in Madrid is cold.
5 They have their holidays in July.
6 My birthday is (on) the 3rd of January.
7 He is free on Saturdays.
8 October is usually a beautiful month.
9 We have to go to Barcelona in May.
10 On Sundays I have dinner with my parents.

CONVERSATION

Juan y Carmen trabajan en la misma oficina
John and Carmen work in the same office

Juan **Oye, Carmen, el sábado doy una pequeña fiesta en mi casa.** Listen, Carmen, on Saturday I am giving a little party at home.
Carmen **¡Ah, qué bien!** How nice!
Juan **Es mi cumpleaños y quiero celebrarlo.** It's my birthday and I want to celebrate.
Carmen **Así que tu cumpleaños es en junio. El mío también. ¡Qué casualidad!** So, your birthday is in June. Mine too. What a coincidence!

Juan   **¿En qué fecha es el tuyo?**   What date is yours?
Carmen   **El dieciocho.**   The eighteenth.
Juan   **Tres días después del mío, entonces. Bueno, ¿puedes venir a mi fiesta?**   Three days after mine, then. Well, can you come to my party?
Carmen   **¿A qué hora es?**   At what time?
Juan   **A las ocho.**   At eight o'clock.
Carmen   **Me gustaría, pero el sábado tengo que trabajar horas extraordinarias hasta las nueve y media.**   I'd like to, but on Saturday I have to work overtime until nine thirty.
Juan   **No te preocupes porque la fiesta dura hasta la una o las dos de la mañana.**   Don't worry because the party goes on until one or two in the morning.
Carmen   **En ese caso acepto. ¿Has invitado a mucha gente?**   In that case I accept. Have you invited many people?
Juan   **No, doce o catorce amigos, porque mi casa no es muy grande. ¿Puedes traer unos discos? Yo tengo solamente unos pocos.**   No, twelve or fourteen friends because my house is not very big. Can you bring some records? I have only a few.
Carmen   **Sí, con mucho gusto.**   Yes, with pleasure.
Juan   **Hasta el sábado, entonces.**   Until Saturday then.
Carmen   **Adiós y gracias por invitarme.**   Good bye and thank you for inviting me.

Lesson 5

31 The verb 'ir' (to go)

This is an irregular verb. Its present tense is as follows:

voy	vamos
vas	vais
va	van

Ir a translates 'to go to' and 'to be going to', e.g.:

Van a la iglesia.   They go to church.
Voy a comprar un periódico.   I am going to buy a newspaper.

The 1st person plural **vamos** translates 'let's' as well as 'we go to' and 'we are going to'. The meaning is usually clear from the context:

Vamos al cine todos los viernes.   We go to the cinema every Friday.
Vamos a comprar los billetes.   We are going to buy the tickets.
Vamos a ver.   Let's see.

Vocabulary

ir de vacaciones	to go on holiday
por	by
tomar	to have (food or drink)
cantar	to sing
descansar	to have a rest
ir de compras	to go shopping
el mercado	the market
el teatro	the theatre

Exercise 19

Translate:
1 We go to church on Sundays.
2 I am going to buy that book.

3 He goes to his friend's house.
4 We go on holiday in the summer.
5 They go to Madrid by train.
6 Let's have a coffee.
7 She is not going to sing.
8 Tomorrow I am going to have a rest.
9 They go shopping in the market.
10 Let's go to the theatre.

32 The past participle

The past participle of regular verbs is formed by adding **-ado** to verbs ending in -ar, and **-ido** to verbs ending in -er and -ir.

hablar→hablado (spoken)
comer→comido (eaten)
vivir→vivido (lived)

There are some irregular past participles. Here are a few examples:

escribir (to write)→**escrito** (written)
ver (to see)→**visto** (seen)
hacer (to do, to make)→**hecho** (done, made)
decir (to say, to tell)→**dicho** (said, told)

33 The perfect tense

This tense is formed with the present indicative of **haber** (to have) followed by the past participle of the appropriate verb. For example, the perfect tense of the verb **comprar** (to buy) is:

he comprado	I have bought
has comprado	you have bought
ha comprado	he has bought
hemos comprado	we have bought
habéis comprado	you have bought
han comprado	they have bought

Haber is an auxiliary verb and is never used as a synonym of **tener**.

The use of the perfect tense in Spanish is similar to that in English:

Hemos viajado todo el día.   We have travelled all day.

Note that the auxiliary and the past participle must not be separated in Spanish:

Siempre he trabajado.   I have always worked.

34 'hay'

'There is' and 'there are' are rendered by **hay,** which is an impersonal form of the verb **haber.** Note that **hay** has no plural:

Hay una barca en la playa.   There is a boat on the beach.
Hay muchos turistas en esta ciudad.   There are many tourists in this town.

Hay que followed by an infinitive is usually translated by 'one must':

Hay que ver la catedral.   One must see the cathedral.
No hay que llorar.   One mustn't cry.

Vocabulary

el azúcar	sugar
el té	tea
nuevo	new
el vestido	dress
terminar	to finish
el trabajo	job, work
ayudar	to help
la naranja	orange
la bolsa	bag
la película	film

Exercise 20

Translate:
1 I have written three letters.
2 They have spoken in Spanish.
3 We have eaten too much.
4 There is sugar in this tea.
5 She has bought a new dress.
6 Have you finished the job?
7 He has never helped in the house.

8 There are some oranges in the bag.
9 Have you (*pol.sing.*) drunk the beer?
10 I haven't seen the film.

35 Personal 'a'

All verbs except **tener** must be followed by the preposition **a** when the direct object is a definite person or animal:

Llamo a Pedro.   I call Peter.
Llamo a mi perro.   I call my dog.
but ...
Tiene un perro.   He has a dog.
Compra el libro.   He buys the book.

Vocabulary

visitar	to visit
llamar	to call
preparar	to prepare
la comida	meal, food
invitar	to invite
casado (-a)	married
el caballo	horse
bañar	to bath
esperar	to wait for, to expect
el profesor	teacher

Exercise 21

Rewrite the following sentences filling in the blanks with the personal 'a' where necessary:
1 Voy a ver ... mi tío.
2 Tenemos que ayudar ... nuestros amigos.
3 Juan ha comprado ... un perro.
4 No he hablado ... el médico.
5 Está leyendo ... el periódico.
6 Vamos a invitar ... Pedro.
7 Tengo ... tres hermanos.

8 Esperamos ... una carta de María.
9 Voy a beber ... una cerveza.
10 Están llamando ... su hija.

Exercise 22

Translate:
1 He visits his mother.
2 I have seen the woman.
3 We have to call the children.
4 María prepares the meal.
5 They have invited their friends.
6 She has a married sister.
7 I am going to buy a horse.
8 We have to bath the dog.
9 They are waiting for the teacher.
10 Carlos has not seen Toledo.

36 Personal pronouns – direct and indirect object

Direct object

me	me
te	you (*fam.*)
le	him, you (*pol.m.*)
la	her, you (*pol.f.*)
lo, la	it (*m.*), it (*f.*)
nos	us
os	you (*fam.*)
les	them, you (*pol.m.*)
las	them, you (*pol.f.*)
los, las	them (*m., f.*) *referring to things.*

Indirect object

me	to me
te	to you
le	to him, to her, to it, to you (*pol.*)
nos	to us
os	to you
les	to them, to you (*pol.*)

Object pronouns usually precede the verb:

Nos ayuda con el trabajo.   He helps us with the work.
Le he escrito una carta.   I have written him a letter.

When the verb is an infinitive, a present participle or an imperative, the pronoun is usually added to the end of the verb:

Tengo que comprarlo.   I have to buy it.
Está esperándome.   He is waiting for me.
Bébalo.   Drink it.

If the infinitive or present participle is preceded by another verb, as in the above examples, the object pronoun may be placed before that verb:

Lo tengo que comprar.   I have to buy it.
Me está esperando.   He is waiting for me.

When an object pronoun is added to the present participle, an accent must be used so that the stress still falls on the same syllable:

Está bebiéndolo.   He is drinking it.
Estamos terminándolo.   We are finishing it.

37 Order of object pronouns

When two object pronouns come together, the indirect object pronoun is always placed first:

Me lo da.   He gives it to me.
Nos la lee.   He reads it to us.

When two pronouns of the third person come together, the indirect object pronoun **le/les** becomes **se**:

Se la envía.   He sends it to him.

In order to avoid any possible ambiguity in the meaning of **le, les** or **se,** you may use **a él, a ellas, a Vd,** etc. after the verb:

Le escribo la carta a él.   I write the letter to him.
Les compro flores a ellas.   I buy them flowers.
Se lo he dado a Vd.   I have given it to you.

Vocabulary

ofrecer	to offer
la taza	cup
enviar	to send
la carne	meat
el pescado	fish
comprender	to understand
vender	to sell
la bicicleta	bicycle

Exercise 23

Replace the words in brackets by the appropriate form of the object pronoun:

1 Juan ofrece (un cigarrillo) (a su amigo).
2 Bebo (una taza de té) por la mañana.
3 Hemos comprado (un coche).
4 Me ha enviado (unas flores).
5 He escrito (una carta) (a mi tía).
6 Comemos (la carne y el pescado).
7 Estos señores no comprenden (el inglés).
8 Tengo que estudiar (la lección).
9 Nos ha vendido (las bicicletas).
10 Hemos dado (los libros) (a Pedro).

38 The imperative mood

(a) In regular verbs, the polite imperative is formed by adding the following endings to the stem:

	sing.	*pl.*	
	-e	**-en**	to verbs ending in -ar
	-a	**-an**	to verbs ending in -er and -ir
hablar	**hable Vd.**	**hablen Vds.**	(speak)
comer	**coma Vd.**	**coman Vds.**	(eat)
subir	**suba Vd.**	**suban Vds.**	(go up)

Vd. is usually added to the polite form of the imperative.

Object pronouns are placed after the imperative unless it is negative:

Bébalo Vd.   Drink it.
No lo beba Vd.   Don't drink it.
Envíeselo Vd.   Send it to him.
No se lo envíe Vd.   Don't send it to him.

(b) In irregular verbs the polite imperative is usually formed by adding the same endings as for regular verbs (above) to the stem of the first person singular of the present indicative:

	Present	*Imperative*
tener (to have)	**tengo**	**tenga Vd./tengan Vds.**
decir (to say)	**digo**	**diga Vd./digan Vds.**
contar (to count)	**cuento**	**cuente Vd./cuenten Vds.**

Exercise 24

Translate:
1 Don't smoke those cigarettes.
2 Drink this wine.
3 Send me the magazine.
4 Read them the letter.
5 Sell him your watch.
6 Learn these numbers.
7 Write your name here.
8 Don't eat those apples.
9 Don't buy that meat.
10 Don't give them to me.

Repeat the exercise, putting the imperative in the plural.

Drills

5 ¿Ha tomado Vd. el café?   Have you had the coffee?
   No, voy a tomarlo ahora.   No, I am going to have it now.

1 ¿Ha tomado Vd. la cerveza?
2 ¿Han ido de compras?
3 ¿Ha escrito la carta?

4 ¿Han hecho Vds. el trabajo?
5 ¿Ha comprado Vd. los cigarrillos?
6 ¿Han visto a su padre?
7 ¿Han terminado Vds. la comida?
8 ¿Ha llamado a Conchita?
9 ¿Ha subido Vd. las maletas?
10 ¿Han bebido Vds. el vino?

6 ¿Preparo la comida? Shall I prepare the meal?
Sí, prepárela. Yes, prepare it.

¿Preparamos la comida? Shall we prepare the meal?
Sí, prepárenla. Yes, prepare it.

1 ¿Compro el periódico?
2 ¿Subimos las maletas?
3 ¿Llamo al profesor?
4 ¿Invitamos a esos amigos?
5 ¿Leo la carta?
6 ¿Enviamos estas flores?
7 ¿Bebo esta cerveza?
8 ¿Vendemos esta bicicleta?

7 Beba Vd. el café. Drink the coffee.
Ya lo he bebido. I have already drunk it.

Beban Vds. el café. Drink the coffee.
Ya lo hemos bebido. We have already drunk it.

1 Prepare Vd. el pescado.
2 Llamen Vds. al perro.
3 Escriba Vd. su nombre.
4 Tomen Vds. la carne.
5 Compre Vd. los billetes.
6 Hablen Vds. a los profesores.
7 Cuente Vd. los libros.
8 Vendan Vds. el reloj.
9 Lea Vd. esta revista.

CONVERSATION

Un día muy ocupado
A very busy day

Carmen **¿Qué vas a hacer hoy?**   What are you going to do today?

Antonio **Hoy tengo varias cosas que hacer. Primero tengo que ir al banco, y después voy a ir a ver a Carlos que está en el hospital.**   Today I have several things to do. First I have to go to the bank, and then I am going to see Charles who is in hospital.

Carmen **¿En el hospital? ¿Qué le pasa?**   In hospital? What is the matter with him?

Antonio **Ha tenido un accidente de automóvil volviendo de Málaga.**   He has had a car accident coming back from Málaga.

Carmen **Y ¿ha sido muy grave?**   And was it very serious?

Antonio **No. Tiene una pierna rota y dos o tres heridas leves.**   No. He has a broken leg and two or three minor injuries.

Carmen **¡Pobre hombre! Tengo que llamar a su mujer y ofrecerle mi ayuda, si la necesita.**   Poor man! I must ring his wife and offer my help if she needs it.

Antonio **Sí, esa es una buena idea.**   Yes, that's a good idea.

Carmen **Bueno, y por la tarde ¿qué vas a hacer?**   Right, and in the afternoon what are you going to do?

Antonio **Tengo que pasarme por la oficina, pero no voy a estar mucho tiempo.**   I have to call in at the office, but I'm not going to be long.

Carmen **Entonces, ¿podemos ir al cine? Ponen una película francesa en el Roxy que deseo ver. Mi hermana la ha visto y me ha dicho que es muy buena.**   In that case can we go to the cinema? They are showing a French film at the Roxy that I want to see. My sister has seen it and she has told me that it is very good.

Antonio **Pues, te espero a las siete menos cuarto a la puerta del cine. ¿Vale?**   So . . . I'll wait for you at a quarter to seven outside the cinema. All right?

Carmen **Muy bien.**   Fine.

Lesson 6

39 Some useful interrogative words

¿Dónde? ¿Adónde?	Where? Where (to)?
¿Cómo?	How?
¿Cuándo?	When?
¿Cuánto, -a, -os, -as?	How much? How many?
¿Por qué?	Why?

Note that **porque** written as one word means 'because'.
¿Verdad? (literally 'true') is used to seek corroboration to a statement:

¿Dónde está la pluma?   Where is the pen?
¿Adónde van Vds.?   Where are you going?
¿Cómo está Vd.?   How are you?
¿Cuándo salimos?   When are we going out?
¿Cuántos libros necesitas?   How many books do you need?
¿Por qué no compras el coche?   Why don't you buy the car?
Porque no tengo dinero.   Because I have no money.
Conchita es muy simpática, ¿verdad?   Conchita is very nice, isn't she?

40 Radical-changing verbs

There are several Spanish verbs which change their stem vowels when the stress falls on them: e changes to **ie**, o changes to **ue** and in some verbs of the third conjugation e changes to **i**.

Present tenses

pensar (to think)	**volver** (to return)	**pedir** (to ask for)
pienso	vuelvo	pido
piensas	vuelves	pides
piensa	vuelve	pide
pensamos	volvemos	pedimos

| pensáis | volvéis | pedís |
| piensan | vuelven | piden |

The first and second persons plural remain regular as the stem vowel is not stressed. Radical changing verbs will be shown in subsequent vocabularies thus: **pensar** (ie); **volver** (ue); **pedir** (i).

41 Reflexive verbs

When the object of the verb is the same person or thing as its subject the verb is called reflexive. These are much more common in Spanish than in English.

Reflexive pronouns

me	myself
te	yourself
se	himself, herself, itself, yourself (*pol.*)
nos	ourselves
os	yourselves
se	themselves, yourselves (*pol.pl.*)

The 3rd person of the reflexive pronoun, **se,** is attached to the infinitive of verbs which are reflexive:

lavarse	to wash oneself
sentarse (ie)	to sit down
dormirse (ue)	to go to sleep

Present tense of **lavarse**

me lavo
te lavas
se lava
nos lavamos
os laváis
se lavan

Regarding their position, reflexive pronouns follow the same rules as object pronouns:

Me lavo.   I wash myself.
Tengo que lavarme.   I have to wash myself.
Estoy lavándome.   I am washing myself.
Lávese Vd.   Wash yourself.
No se lave Vd.   Don't wash yourself.

Some verbs change their meaning when used reflexively:

llamar	to call
llamarse	to call oneself, to be called
ir	to go
irse	to go away
dormir	to sleep
dormirse	to go to sleep
llevar	to carry, to wear
llevarse	to take away

With some verbs the reflexive pronoun may be used to give emphasis or finality to the action of the verb:

decidir, decidirse a	to decide
morir, morirse	to die
parar, pararse	to stop

42 Reciprocal form

The reflexive pronoun is also used in reciprocal verbs such as:

quererse (ie)	to love each other
comprenderse	to understand each other
verse	to see each other

Mi hermano y yo no nos comprendemos.   My brother and I don't understand each other.

Vocabulary

todos los días	every day
casarse	to get married
odiar (se)	to hate (each other)
ayudar (se)	to help (each other)
acostarse (ue)	to go to bed

Exercise 25

Translate:

1 Pedro and Anita write to each other every day.
2 The car is going to stop.
3 We are going to get married.
4 The children go to bed at eight o'clock.
5 We have to wash ourselves.
6 The two men hate each other.
7 He always asks me for money.
8 They never help each other.
9 Carlos returns from the office at half past six.
10 I must go to sleep.
11 Take away these cups!
12 The street is called Baeza.
13 I am going to sit here.
14 We are going away tomorrow.
15 I have decided to live in Spain.

43 Personal pronouns with prepositions (disjunctive)

After prepositions the same forms as those of the subject pronouns are used, except for:

mí (me); **ti** (you, *familiar*); **sí** (himself, herself, yourself)

Estas cartas son para mí.   These letters are for me.
No vuelve con nosotros.   He does not come back with us.
Vamos sin ella.   We go without her.

With the preposition **con** ('with') the forms **mí, ti,** and **sí** become **conmigo, contigo** and **consigo:**

No puedo vivir contigo   I cannot live with you.
Siempre lleva un libro consigo   He always carries a book with him (self).

When **consigo** is not reflexive, the forms 'with him', 'with her', 'with you', 'with them', are translated by **con él, con ella, con Vd.,** etc.

Vocabulary

con	with
el regalo	present
para	for
el tiempo	weather
contra	against
sin	without
siempre	always
el viaje	journey
entre	between
según	according to

Exercise 26

Translate:
1 We are working with them.
2 He has bought a present for me.
3 Is he going to come back with you (*pol.s.*)?
4 The weather is against us.
5 They have gone away without him.
6 He has always lived with me.
7 These letters are for her.
8 They are going to buy the house between them.
9 Are the children with you (*fam. s.*)?
10 According to him, the journey is too long.

44 Irregular verbs in the present tense

In their present tenses the following verbs are irregular only in the
first person singular:

poner (to put)	**pongo,** pones, pone, ponemos, ponéis, ponen
salir (to go out)	**salgo,** sales, sale, salimos, salís, salen
ver (to see)	**veo,** ves, ve, vemos, veis, ven
hacer (to do, to make)	**hago,** haces, hace, hacemos, hacéis, hacen
traer (to bring)	**traigo,** traes, trae, traemos, traéis, traen
dar (to give)	**doy,** das, da, damos, dais, dan
saber (to know)	**sé,** sabes, sabe, sabemos, sabéis, saben

45 Idiomatic uses of 'hacer'

Besides translating 'to do', 'to make', **hacer** is used:

a) in certain impersonal expressions relating to the weather
¿Qué tiempo hace?   What's the weather like?
Hace frío.   It's cold.
Hace (mucho) calor.   It's (very) hot.
Hace sol.   It's sunny.
Hace viento.   It's windy.
Hace buen día.   It's a nice day.

b) in certain expressions of time
Hace muchos años.   Many years ago.
Hace media hora.   Half an hour ago.
¿Hace mucho tiempo que esperas?   Have you been waiting long?

46 Impersonal verbs

llover (ue)	to rain
nevar (ie)	to snow
helar (ie)	to freeze
tronar (ue)	to thunder
amanecer	to dawn
anochecer	to get dark

47 The verb 'gustar'

This verb translates 'to like', 'to be keen on', but in the Spanish construction the English subject becomes the indirect object and the English object becomes the subject.

Me gusta el café.   I like coffee.
Nos gusta Inglaterra.   We like England.
Les gustan las uvas.   They like grapes.
A Carlos le gusta pintar.   Carlos likes painting.

When the subject of **gustar** is a verb, as in the sentence **A Carlos le gusta pintar,** the infinitive must always be used. Note also that the preposition **a** must be used in front of the noun which is the indirect object.

Sometimes a disjunctive pronoun is used for emphasis or to indicate a contrast. For example:

¿A Vd. le gusta el flamenco?   Do *you* like flamenco?
A mí no me gustan los deportes, pero a mi marido le gustan mucho.   I don't like sports, but my husband likes them very much.

Exercise 27

Translate:
 1 What is the weather like?
 2 Today it's very cold.
 3 It's going to rain tomorrow.
 4 I don't like this beer.
 5 He is going to bring us coffee.
 6 He likes to go out every evening.
 7 I don't know where it is.
 8 They go to Spain because they like the sun.
 9 Twenty five years ago.
10 Carmen likes to sit in the garden.

48 The verb 'querer' (ie)

This verb means 'to love' (a person or animal) or 'to want', 'to wish'. It must not be confused with **gustar**, although the form **quisiera** (imperfect subjunctive) often translates the English 'I should like':

Quiero a mis hijos.   I love my children.
No quieren ir a Francia.   They don't want to go to France.
Quisiera ver a Ramón.   I should like to see Ramón.

Drills

 8 ¿Les gusta a Vds. España? Do you like Spain?
    Sí, nos gusta mucho. Yes, we like it very much.

 1 ¿Le gusta a Vd. la playa?
 2 ¿Le gustan a Carlos los deportes?
 3 ¿Les gusta a Vds. vivir en Madrid?

4 ¿Os gusta la cerveza?
5 ¿Le gusta a Conchita el regalo?
6 ¿Te gustan los niños?
7 ¿Le gusta a Vd. viajar?
8 ¿Les gusta a tus amigos el vino?
9 ¿Les gusta a Vds. el hotel?
10 ¿Les gusta a ellos el pescado?

9 Van Vds. con Carlos ¿verdad?   You are going with Carlos, aren't you?
Sí, vamos con él. Yes, we are going with him.

1 Trabaja Vd. con María ¿verdad?
2 Esta carta es para nosotros ¿verdad?
3 Su hermano vuelve con Vd. ¿verdad?
4 Vamos al teatro sin los niños ¿verdad?
5 Estas flores son para mí ¿verdad?
6 Vive con sus padres ¿verdad?
7 Estos periódicos son para Vds. ¿verdad?
8 Va Vd. de compras sin su marido ¿verdad?

10 ¿Quiere Vd. acostarse?   Do you want to go to bed?
Sí, quisiera acostarme. Yes, I should like to go to bed.

¿Quieren Vds. acostarse?   Do you want to go to bed?
Si, quisiéramos acostarnos. Yes, we should like to go to bed.

1 ¿Quiere Vd. sentarse?
2 ¿Quiere Vd. lavarse?
3 ¿Quiere Vd. dormirse?
4 ¿Quiere Vd. irse?
5 ¿Quiere Vd. pararse?
6 ¿Quieren Vds. sentarse?
7 ¿Quieren Vds. lavarse?
8 ¿Quieren Vds. dormirse?
9 ¿Quieren Vds. irse?
10 ¿Quieren Vds. pararse?

CONVERSATION

Planes de vacaciones
Holiday plans

Miguel **¿Adónde van Vds. de vacaciones este año?** Where are you going on holiday this year?

Pilar **Vamos a un pueblo de la costa del Mediterráneo, cerca de Valencia.** We are going to a village on the Mediterranean coast, near Valencia.

Miguel **¿En qué mes van Vds.?** Which month do you go?

Pilar **Vamos en julio porque hace muy buen tiempo. Hace calor y el mar está delicioso para bañarse.** We go in July because the weather is very good. It's warm and the sea is lovely to bathe in.

Miguel **A nosotros nos gusta más el norte. Todos los años vamos a Santander en agosto.** We like the north better. Every year we go to Santander in August.

Pilar **Pero en el norte hace mal tiempo, llueve mucho y hay muchos días en los que es imposible ir a la playa.** But in the north the weather is bad, it rains a lot and there are many days when it's impossible to go to the beach.

Miguel **Es verdad. Pero no vamos buscando el sol, vamos huyendo del calor de Madrid que en agosto es insoportable.** It's true. But we are not seeking the sun, we are running away from the heat in Madrid which, in August, is unbearable.

Pilar **Pues, a mí me gusta el calor. Ya tenemos bastante frío todo el invierno.** Well, I like the hot weather. We are cold enough all through the winter.

Miguel **Yo, sin embargo, prefiero el invierno al verano.** I, on the other hand, prefer winter to summer.

Pilar **Sobre gustos no hay nada escrito.** There is no accounting for tastes.

Lesson 7

49 The imperfect tense

The imperfect is used to express an habitual action, an action repeated over an indefinite period of time, with no beginning and no end. It translates the English 'was doing', 'used to do', sometimes 'did' and also 'would' in the sense of 'used to'.

Imperfect tenses

hablar	**comer**	**vivir**
hablaba	comía	vivía
hablabas	comías	vivías
hablaba	comía	vivía
hablábamos	comíamos	vivíamos
hablabais	comíais	vivíais
hablaban	comían	vivían

Carlos compraba el periódico todos los días.   Carlos used to buy the newspaper every day.
El hombre vendía caramelos.   The man was selling sweets.

As the first and third persons singular have the same forms, the subject pronoun is sometimes used to avoid ambiguity.

There are only three verbs which are irregular in the imperfect tense:

ser (to be)	**ir** (to go)	**ver** (to see)
era	iba	veía
eras	ibas	veías
era	iba	veía
éramos	íbamos	veíamos
erais	ibais	veíais
eran	iban	veían

Íbamos a España una vez al año.   We used to go to Spain once a year.

The forms 'there was', 'there were' are translated by **había** (the imperfect of the verb **haber**):

Había mucha gente en la playa.   There were a lot of people on the beach.

Había un embotellamiento en la plaza.   There was a traffic jam in the square.

50 The verb 'soler' (ue)

This is a defective verb only used in the present and imperfect indicative. It translates 'to be in the habit of' and expressions with 'generally', 'usually', 'as a rule':

Suelo levantarme a las siete.   I usually get up at seven.

Solíamos ir de paseo los domingos.   We used to go for a walk on Sundays.

51 The pluperfect tense

This is a compound tense and is formed with the imperfect of the auxiliary **haber** and the past participle of the appropriate verb. Thus:

Habíamos comido.   We had eaten.

Habían escrito.   They had written.

Ramón había salido.   Ramón had gone out.

Vocabulary

el gerente	manager
los bombones	chocolates
el muchacho	boy
buscar	to look for
la maleta	suitcase
la representación	performance
empezar (ie)	to begin
la fábrica	factory
el mar	sea
mirar	to look at

Exercise 28

Translate:
1 Luis was smoking a cigarette.
2 I usually see her in the morning.
3 They had spoken to the hotel manager.
4 He used to bring me chocolates.
5 The boy was looking for his suitcase.
6 The performance used to start at ten o'clock.
7 He had worked in a factory.
8 The sea was very cold.
9 The woman was looking at us.
10 We usually ate a lot of fish.

52 Negatives

jamás, nunca	never
nada	nothing
tampoco	neither
nadie	no one, nobody
ninguno (-a)	none
ni ... ni	neither ... nor

Nunca sale de casa.   He never goes out of the house.
Nadie lo había visto.   Nobody had seen it.
Ni fuma, ni bebe.   He neither smokes, nor drinks.

However, the double negative is more common in Spanish:

No necesito nada.   I don't need anything.
Mi padre no lo sabe tampoco.   My father doesn't know either.
No escribe nunca.   He never writes.

Ninguno (-a) can play the role of adjective or pronoun. It may refer to people or things and it is always used in the singular. As an adjective the masculine form shortens to **ningún** in front of the noun:

No hay ningún niño en la playa.   There aren't any children on the beach.
Voy a comprar cigarrillos, no tengo ninguno.   I am going to buy cigarettes, I haven't any.

Corresponding to these negatives, there are the affirmative forms:

siempre	always
algo	something
también	also, too
alguien	someone, somebody
alguno (-a)	some, any
o ... o	either ... or

Alguno, like its opposite **ninguno,** shortens to **algún** in front of the masculine noun. It may sometimes be used in the singular when a plural form would be usual in English.

Quiero comprar algún periódico inglés.   I want to buy some English newspapers.
Alguien ha preguntado por Vd.   Somebody has asked for you.
O canta, o baila.   Either he sings, or he dances.

Vocabulary

conocer	to know
el pan	bread
la leche	milk
venir (ie)	to come
leer	to read
poder	to be able
ocurrir	to happen

Exercise 29

Fill in the blanks with the appropriate negative word:
1 Juan no quiere hacer ......
2 No conocemos a ...... en esta ciudad.
3 No tienen ...... pan ...... leche.
4 María no viene ...... a verme.
5 No he leído ...... libro de Cervantes.
6 Carlos no puede ir y su hermano ......
7 ...... sabe lo que ha ocurrido.
8 No hay ...... nuevo.
9 No hemos comprado ...... revista.
10 Esa mujer no ha trabajado ......

53 Adverbs

Many adverbs are formed in Spanish by adding the ending -**mente** to the feminine form of the adjective:

maravillosamente wonderfully
fácilmente easily
frecuentemente frequently

When two or more adverbs ending in -**mente** follow one another, only the last one ends in -**mente**; the others keep the feminine form of the adjective:

El niño ha sido castigado justa y severamente. The boy has been punished justly and severely.

Exercise 30

Form adverbs from the following adjectives:
1 feliz (happy).
2 verdadero (true).
3 triste (sad).
4 lento (slow).
5 nuevo (new).
6 agradable (pleasant).
7 malo (bad).
8 cierto (certain).
9 rápido (fast).
10 claro (clear).

54 Comparison of adjectives and adverbs

The comparison of equality 'as . . . as' is rendered by **tan . . . como**:

Carlos es tan alto como Pedro. Carlos is as tall as Pedro.
Nadie habla tan despacio como Juan. Nobody talks as slowly as Juan.

The comparison of inequality ('more . . . than', 'less . . . than') is rendered by **más . . . que, menos . . . que**:

Yo soy más pobre que Vd. I am poorer than you.

María es menos inteligente que su hermana. María is less intelligent than her sister.

Mi mujer ha llegado más tarde que yo. My wife has arrived later than I.

Este hombre trabaja menos diligentemente que aquél. This man works less diligently than that one.

55 Irregular comparison of adjectives

bueno (good)	→**mejor** (better)
malo (bad)	→**peor** (worse)
mucho (a lot of)	→**más** (more)
poco (little, few)	→**menos** (less, fewer)
grande (big)	→**mayor** (bigger, older)
pequeño (small)	→**menor** (smaller, younger)

Grande and **pequeño** also have a regular comparison, **más grande** and **más pequeño,** which refers only to size:

Esta casa es más grande que la mía. This house is bigger than mine.

Mejor, peor, mayor and **menor** have a plural form ending in **-es,** for masculine and feminine.

56 Irregular comparison of adverbs

bien (well)	→**mejor** (better)
mal (badly)	→**peor** (worse)
mucho (much)	→**más** (more)
poco (little)	→**menos** (less)

Pilar canta mal, pero yo canto peor que ella. Pilar sings badly, but I sing worse than she does.

57 Comparison of nouns

The comparison of inequality has the same forms as that of adjectives and adverbs: **más . . . que, menos . . . que:**

Carmen tiene más paciencia que Pilar. Carmen has more patience than Pilar.

Tengo menos libros que tú. I have fewer books than you.

The comparison of equality is expressed by **tanto . . . como. Tanto** is an adjective and has to agree in gender and number with the following noun:

No he bebido tanto vino como Pedro. I haven't drunk as much wine as Pedro.

Vd. no recibe tantas cartas como yo. You don't receive as many letters as I do.

Vocabulary

fuerte	strong
el jerez	sherry
seco	dry
negro	black
el zapato	shoe
azul	blue
pronto	soon
necesitar	to need
el agua (*f.*)	water
caliente	hot, warm
la piscina	swimming pool

Exercise 31

Translate:
1 My brother is stronger than I.
2 This sherry is drier than that one.
3 Carlos is three years older than María.
4 The black shoes are smaller than the blue (ones).
5 His car is better than mine.
6 He writes worse than his sister.
7 I have arrived sooner than my father.
8 They haven't as much money as their friends.
9 I don't need as many suitcases as you.
10 The water in the pool is warmer than in the sea.

Drills

11 ¿Iban Vds. al mercado?   Did you go to the market?
Sí, solíamos ir. Yes, we used to go.

¿Leía Vd. el periódico?   Did you read the paper?
Sí, solía leerlo.   Yes, I used to read it.

1 ¿Veía Vd. a Carmen?
2 ¿Comían en el hotel?
3 ¿Trabajaban Vds.?
4 ¿Escribía Vd. cartas?
5 ¿Viajaba a Londres?
6 ¿Iban Vds. al café?
7 ¿Hablaba Vd. español?
8 ¿Invitaba a sus amigos?
9 ¿Tenían dinero?
10 ¿Bebía Vd. vino?

12 ¿Ha venido alguien?   Has anyone come?
No, no ha venido nadie.   No, nobody has come.

1 ¿Quiere Vd. algo?
2 ¿Han vivido aquí siempre?
3 ¿Quieren Vds. té o café?
4 ¿Hay algún turista inglés?
5 ¿Conocen Vds. a alguien?
6 ¿Tiene Vd. alguna revista española?

13 Mi casa es pequeña.   My house is small.
La mía es más pequeña.   Mine is smaller.

1 Mis libros son viejos.
2 Mi coche es malo.
3 Mi jardín es bonito.
4 Mi hotel es bueno.
5 Mi marido es alto.
6 Mis zapatos son caros.
7 Mis maletas son grandes.
8 Mis cigarrillos son baratos.

CONVERSATION

El Sr. Sánchez habla con su secretaria
Mr. Sánchez speaks with his secretary

Sr. Sánchez	**Buenos días, Lolita. Llego más tarde que de costumbre.** Good morning, Lolita. I'm later than usual.
Lolita	**Sí. ¿Qué le ha ocurrido? Son casi las diez.** Yes. What's happened to you? It's almost ten o'clock.
Sr. Sánchez	**El coche no arrancaba esta mañana. Como ha helado durante la noche, el motor estaba muy frío.** The car wouldn't start this morning. As it has been freezing during the night, the engine was very cold.
Lolita	**¡Qué lata! Por eso yo nunca vengo en el coche. Uso el Metro. Es mucho más rápido y me ahorro muchos problemas.** What a nuisance! That is why I never come in the car. I use the Underground. It's much quicker and I save myself a lot of problems.
Sr. Sánchez	**Claro. Así no tiene Vd. gastos ni de gasolina ni de aparcamiento. Yo creo que voy a hacer lo mismo pronto.** Of course. That way you have no expenses of either petrol or parking. I think I am going to do the same soon.
Lolita	**Es lo mejor. No lo dude.** It's the best thing. Believe me.
Sr. Sánchez	**¿Ha venido alguien?** Has anyone called?
Lolita	**No. No ha venido nadie.** No. Nobody has called.
Sr. Sánchez	**Y, ¿hay algún recado?** And are there any messages?
Lolita	**No, nada. Hay algunas cartas que he dejado en su escritorio.** No, nothing. There are some letters that I have left on your desk.
Sr. Sánchez	**Bueno. Entonces, voy a ver el correo, y dentro de media hora venga Vd. a mi despacho porque quiero dictarle unas cartas.** All right. I'm going to see the post, then; and in half an hour come to my office, because I want to dictate a few letters.
Lolita	**Muy bien, Sr. Sánchez.** Very well, Mr. Sánchez.

Lesson 8

58 Shortening of adjectives

The following adjectives have shortened forms:

a) before the masculine noun

bueno (good)	**buen**
malo (bad)	**mal**
alguno (some)	**algún**
ninguno (none)	**ningún**
primero (first)	**primer**
tercero (third)	**tercer**
uno (one)	**un**

b) before nouns of either gender

grande (big)	**gran**
ciento (one hundred)	**cien**
cualquiera (any)	**cualquier**

Un buen libro. A good book.
Una buena película. A good film.
El primer tren. The first train.
La primera fila. The first row.
Cualquier autobús. Any bus.
Cualquier persona. Any person.

59 Position of adjectives

Adjectives in Spanish usually follow the noun, but there are some exceptions. Adjectives which *always precede* the noun are:

a) adjectives of quantity

mucho	a lot of
poco	little

tanto	so much
cuanto	how much
demasiado	too much
bastante	enough

b) indefinite adjectives

alguno	some, any
ninguno	none
cada	each
otro	other
todo	all
tal	such

Cada is an invariable word:
Cada hombre y cada mujer.   Each man and each woman.

Otro is never preceded by the indefinite article:
Otro hombre y otra mujer.   Another man and another woman.

Tal is invariable and never followed by the indefinite article:
Tal hombre y tal mujer.   Such a man and such a woman.

c) numerals (cardinal and ordinal) – but see section 25 for exceptions.

d) Some common adjectives like **bueno** (good), **malo** (bad), **pequeño** (small), **hermoso** (beautiful), **joven** (young) and **viejo** (old) often precede the noun.
Un hermoso paisaje.   A beautiful landscape.
Un joven guitarrista.   A young guitarist.

Certain adjectives change their meaning according to their position:
grande – Una casa grande.   A big house.
but – **Una gran mujer.**   A great (famous) woman.

nuevo – Un coche nuevo.   A (brand) new car.
but – **Un nuevo coche.**   A new (different) car.

pobre – Un hombre pobre.   A poor (impecunious) man.
but – **Un pobre hombre.**   An unfortunate man.

mismo – El mismo hombre.   The same man.
but – **El hombre mismo.**   The man himself.

In spite of all these rules, the position of adjectives in Spanish is fairly flexible and is often determined by emphasis, balance and style; observation and practice will help the student to overcome any initial difficulties.

Vocabulary

el pintor	painter
llevar	to wear, to carry
la ropa	clothes
la zona	area
perder (ie)	to lose
el bolso	handbag
el sombrero	hat
la bebida	drink
el sello	stamp
el nadador	swimmer

Exercise 32

Translate
1 We have had a good journey.
2 Each man had a job.
3 He is a great painter.
4 They always wear the same clothes.
5 There are enough hotels in this area.
6 The poor woman has lost her handbag.
7 I have a brand new hat.
8 We have asked for another drink.
9 These stamps are very old.
10 All the children are good swimmers.

60 Present tense of three irregular verbs

venir (to come)	**oir** (to hear)	**decir** (to say, to tell)
vengo	oigo	digo
vienes	oyes	dices
viene	oye	dice
venimos	oímos	decimos
venís	oís	decís
vienen	oyen	dicen

61 Some irregular past participles

(See section 32 for others)

abrir (to open)	→**abierto**
decir (so say)	→**dicho**
poner (to put)	→**puesto**
romper (to break)	→**roto**
volver (to return)	→**vuelto**
describir (to describe)	→**descrito**

62 The future tense

The future tense of regular verbs is formed by adding the following endings to the infinitive: **-é, -ás, -á, -emos, eís, -án.**

hablar (to speak)	**comer** (to eat)	**vivir** (to live)
hablar**é**	comer**é**	vivir**é**
hablar**ás**	comer**ás**	vivir**ás**
hablar**á**	comer**á**	vivir**á**
hablar**emos**	comer**emos**	vivir**emos**
hablar**éis**	comer**éis**	vivir**éis**
hablar**án**	comer**án**	vivir**án**

Hablaremos en español todo el tiempo. We shall speak Spanish all the time.
Comerá con nosotros mañana. He will eat with us tomorrow.
Vivirán cerca de sus padres. They will live near his parents.

63 Irregular verbs in the future tense

A few verbs are irregular in the future tense. The endings remain the same as for regular verbs, but the *stem* changes:

caber (to fit in)	ca*b*ré, ca*b*rás, etc.
decir (to say)	d*i*ré, d*i*rás, etc.
haber (to have)	ha*b*ré, ha*b*rás, etc.
hacer (to do)	ha*r*é, ha*r*ás, etc.
poder (to be able)	po*d*ré, po*d*rás, etc.
poner (to put)	pon*d*ré, pon*d*rás, etc.
querer (to want)	que*r*ré, que*r*rás, etc.
saber (to know)	sa*b*ré, sa*b*rás, etc.
salir (to go out)	sal*d*ré, sal*d*rás, etc.
tener (to have)	ten*d*ré, ten*d*rás, etc.
valer (to be worth)	val*d*ré, val*d*rás, etc.
venir (to come)	ven*d*ré, ven*d*rás, etc.

No podremos ir.   We shall not be able to go.
Diré unas pocas palabras.   I shall say a few words.
Vendrán con él.   They will come with him.

64 The conditional

The conditional is formed by adding to the infinitive the following endings: **-ía, -ías, -ía, -íamos, -íais, -ían.**

hablar	**comer**	**vivir**
hablaría	comería	viviría
hablarías	comerías	vivirías
hablaría	comería	viviría
hablaríamos	comeríamos	viviríamos
hablaríais	comeríais	viviríais
hablarían	comerían	vivirían

As the first and third persons singular have the same forms, the subject pronoun is sometimes used to avoid ambiguity:

Me gustaría ir a la fiesta.   I should like to go to the party.
No vivirían en España.   They would not live in Spain.

65 Irregular verbs in the conditional

Verbs which are irregular in the future tense are also irregular in the conditional with the same *stem* change:

decir→di*ría*; **hacer**→ha*ría*; **tener**→ten*dría*; **venir**→ven*dría*, etc.

Yo quería saber lo que diría.   I wanted to know what he would say.

Tendrían que pagar el daño.   They would have to pay the damage.

66 Other uses of the future and the conditional

The future and the conditional may be used to express probability or assumption:

¿Por qué no ha venido Pedro?   Why hasn't Pedro come?
Estará enfermo.   He is probably ill.
¿Cuántos años tenía el niño?   How old was the boy?
Tendría nueve años.   He must have been nine.

'Will' and 'would' expressing will or determination are translated by **querer**:

No quiere contestar el teléfono.   He will not answer the phone.
No quería venir con nosotros.   He would not come with us.
¿Quiere Vd. un café?   Will you have a coffee?
¿Quiere Vd. cerrar la puerta, por favor?   Will you shut the door, please?

Vocabulary

próximo	next
temprano	early
esta noche	tonight
conducir	to drive
andar	to walk
lejos	far
el museo	museum
el autocar	coach

Exercise 33

Translate:
1 They will get married next month.
2 I shall go to bed early tonight.
3 He will come with us on holiday.
4 We shall visit them on Sunday.
5 They will not speak to us.
6 It would be better to stop.
7 I shouldn't like to drive a big car.
8 He won't have to walk very far.
9 They wouldn't be worth anything.
10 We shan't be able to see the museum.
11 He would not sell the house.
12 The coach will leave at eight o'clock.

67 Verbs with prepositions

A verb preceded by a preposition must always be an infinitive:

Le veré antes de salir.   I'll see him before leaving.
Se ha ido sin hablar con nosotros.   He has left without speaking to us.

Vocabulary

cerrar (ie)	to close
la ventana	window
antes de	before
después de	after
de	of, from
pasar	to spend (time)
llorar	to cry
sentirse (ie)	to feel
enfermo	ill
el marisco	seafood
la habitación	room
tomar	to take
la voz	voice

ronco (-a)	hoarse
gritar	to shout
enseñar	to show

Exercise 34

Translate

1 Close the windows before going to bed.
2 I shall have to think before deciding.
3 You cannot go without finishing the job.
4 He has spent the day without speaking to anyone.
5 She was crying without knowing why.
6 They were feeling ill after eating seafood.
7 I was very sleepy after working all night.
8 We should like to see the room before taking it.
9 His voice was hoarse from shouting so much.
10 After writing the letter show it to me.

68 Idiomatic uses of 'llevar' and 'hacer'

Llevar (to wear, to carry) and **hacer** (to do, to make) are often used to express how long an action has or had been going on:

¿Cuánto tiempo lleva Vd. en España?   How long have you been in Spain?
Hace tres meses que estoy aquí.   I have been here three months.
¿Cuánto tiempo llevan Vds. esperando?   How long have you been waiting?
Hace media hora que esperamos.   We have been waiting half an hour.

Question and answer can be reversed thus:

¿Cuánto tiempo hace que está Vd. en España?
Llevo tres meses aquí.
¿Cuánto tiempo hace que esperan Vds?
Llevamos media hora esperando.

Drills

14 ¿Ha venido tu amigo?   Has your friend come?
No, vendrá luego.   No, he will come later.

¿Ha leído Vd. el periódico?   Have you read the newspaper?
No, lo leeré luego.   No, I shall read it later.

1 ¿Han visto a su padre?
2 ¿Han terminado Vds. el trabajo?
3 ¿Ha ido Vd. al banco?
4 ¿Ha escrito Pedro la carta?
5 ¿Han enviado Vds. las flores?
6 ¿Han cerrado la tienda?
7 ¿Ha salido Juan?
8 ¿Ha hecho Vd. la comida?
9 ¿Han visto las habitaciones?
10 ¿Ha abierto Vd. las ventanas?

15 *Study the examples in section 68, then do the following drill:*
1 ¿Cuánto tiempo lleva Vd. estudiando español?
......seis meses......
2 ¿Cuánto tiempo llevan Vds. en Madrid?
......tres años......
3 ¿Cuánto tiempo llevan ellos trabajando aquí?
......dos semanas......
4 ¿Cuánto tiempo lleva Juan viviendo en Londres?
......un año......
5 ¿Cuánto tiempo lleva Vd. esperando?
......diez minutos......
6 ¿Cuánto tiempo hace que estudia Vd. español?
......seis meses......
7 ¿Cuánto tiempo hace que están Vds. en Madrid?
......tres años......
8 ¿Cuánto tiempo hace que ellos trabajan aquí?
......dos semanas......
9 ¿Cuánto tiempo hace que Juan vive en Londres?
......un año......
10 ¿Cuánto tiempo hace que espera Vd.?
......diez minutos......

CONVERSATION

Un encuentro en la calle
A chance meeting in the street

Pedro	**Teresa, ¡cuanto tiempo sin vernos!** Teresa, we haven't met for a long time!
Teresa	**¿Cómo estás?** How are you?
Pedro	**Muy bien, gracias. Y tú ¿qué haces en Madrid? ¿No vivías en Sevilla?** Very well, thank you. And you, what are you doing in Madrid? Weren't you living in Seville?
Teresa	**Ya no. Mi marido está trabajando aquí ahora. Llevamos tres meses en Madrid.** No longer. My husband is working here now. We have been in Madrid three months.
Pedro	**¡Ah, muy bien! ¿Habéis encontrado piso ya?** Oh, very good! Have you found a flat yet?
Teresa	**No. De momento estamos viviendo con los padres de Antonio. Pero el piso no es muy grande y estamos un poco apretados.** No. At the moment we are living with Antonio's parents. But the flat is not very big and we are a little cramped.
Pedro	**¿Qué tipo de piso buscáis? Porque tengo un amigo que vende uno con tres dormitorios, salón, comedor, cocina y baño. Y también tiene una terraza bastante grande. Lo que no sé es lo que pide. ¿Crees que puede interesarte?** What sort of flat are you looking for? Because I have a friend who is selling one with three bedrooms, lounge, dining room, kitchen and bathroom. It also has quite a large balcony. What I don't know is how much he is asking. Do you think it may interest you?
Teresa	**Ya lo creo. Si el precio es razonable. ¿Cómo podemos ponernos en contacto con él?** Yes, indeed. If the price is reasonable. How can we get in touch with him.?
Pedro	**Se llama Alberto Solís, y estos son su teléfono y sus señas.** His name is Alberto Solís, and this is his phone number and address.
Teresa	**Pues, muchísimas gracias, Pedro. A ver si tenemos suerte.** Well, thank you very much, Pedro. Let's see if we are lucky.
Pedro	**Eso espero. Hasta pronto.** I hope so. See you soon.
Teresa	**Sí. Te llamaremos. Adiós.** Yes. We'll call you. 'Bye.

Lesson 9

69 The past historic

The past historic is used to express a completed action, an action that took place within a definite period of time.

hablar	comer	vivir
hablé	comí	viví
hablaste	comiste	viviste
habló	comió	vivió
hablamos	comimos	vivimos
hablasteis	comisteis	vivisteis
hablaron	comieron	vivieron

Ayer hablé con Carmen. Yesterday I spoke to Carmen.
Comieron sopa y pescado. They ate soup and fish.
Vivió en Madrid diez años. He lived in Madrid ten years.

70 Irregular verbs in the past historic

There is an important group of verbs which are irregular in the past historic (sometimes called the past definite). The endings are the same for all of them but the *stem* changes. Here are three examples (the stem changes being italicised):

andar (to walk)	**hacer** (to do, to make)	**venir** (to come)
anduve	hice	vine
anduviste	hiciste	viniste
anduvo	hizo	vino
anduvimos	hicimos	vinimos
anduvisteis	hicisteis	vinisteis
anduvieron	hicieron	vinieron

Other verbs belonging to the same group are listed below, with their irregular stems:

estar (to be)	est*uv*-
decir (to say)	d*ij*-
saber (to know)	s*up*-
poner (to put)	p*us*-
poder (to be able)	p*ud*-
conducir (to drive)	condu*j*-
querer (to want)	qu*is*-
haber (to have)	h*ub*-
tener (to have)	t*uv*-
traer (to bring)	tra*j*-

No quiso abrir la puerta.   He didn't want to open the door.
Estuve enfermo dos meses.   I was ill for two months.
No pudieron venir juntos.   They weren't able to come together.

Note that the 3rd person plural of **decir, conducir, traer** is **dijeron, condujeron, trajeron** (the 'i' of the ending is omitted after the 'j').

71 Past historic of 'ser' and 'ir'

Ser and **ir** have the same irregular forms in the past historic:

fui	**fuimos**
fuiste	**fuisteis**
fue	**fueron**

El verano pasado fui a Mallorca.   Last summer I went to Mallorca.
Fue un hombre muy famoso.   He was a very famous man.

72 Past historic of 'dar' (to give)

di	**dimos**
diste	**disteis**
dio	**dieron**

Me dio un recado para Vd.   He gave me a message for you.
Les di tres mil pesetas.   I gave them three thousand pesetas.

73 Radical-changing verbs in the past historic

There is a small group of verbs ending in -ir which are irregular in
the 3rd persons (singular and plural) of the past historic. The 'e' in
the stem becomes 'i' and the 'o' becomes 'u'. The rest of the tense is
regular. Here are some examples:

	3rd pers. sing.	3rd pers. pl.
seguir (to follow)	siguió	siguieron
pedir (to ask for)	pidió	pidieron
sentir (to feel)	sintió	sintieron
dormir (to sleep)	durmió	durmieron
morir (to die)	murió	murieron

Durmió solamente cuatro horas.   He slept only four hours.
Pidieron dos botellas de vino.   They asked for two bottles of wine.

Vocabulary

dar un paseo	to go for a walk
por	along
el río	river
el sobre	envelope
pagar	to pay
la comida	meal
el cheque	cheque
el camarero	waiter
el kilómetro	kilometre
la hora de comer	lunch time

Exercise 35

Translate:
1 We went for a walk along the river.
2 They didn't want to see me.
3 I put the letter in the envelope.
4 He died two years later.
5 He paid for the meal with a cheque.
6 The waiter brought us the drinks and went away.

7 They walked five kilometres looking for a garage.
8 I went out at ten o'clock and returned at lunch time.
9 We told him that his father had arrived.
10 He didn't do anything all morning.

74 Imperfect and past historic contrasted

It is sometimes difficult for the student to decide whether to use the
imperfect or the past historic, since, at times, they can be both
translated by the English 'did'. Remember that the imperfect tells us
what was going on, what somebody was doing or used to do over an
indefinite period of time, whereas the past historic expresses what
happened or what somebody did at a particular time.
Study the following examples:

Nadábamos en el río todos los días.   We swam (used to swim) in
the river every day.
Ayer nadamos en el río.   Yesterday we swam in the river.
Siempre fumaba un puro después de cenar.   He always smoked
(used to smoke) a cigar after dinner.
Anoche fumó un puro después de cenar.   Last night he smoked a
cigar after dinner.
Llovía cuando salimos del hotel.   It was raining when we left the
hotel.
Llovió toda la tarde.   It rained all afternoon.

Vocabulary

la ducha	shower
sonar (ue)	to sound, to ring
jugar (ue)	to play
mientras	while
bajar	to go down
la cuenta	bill
hacer la maleta	to pack
cansado (-a)	tired
la (tarjeta) postal	postcard
el policía	policeman
preguntar	to ask

Exercise 36

Change the infinitives in brackets into the correct form of the imperfect or past historic as appropriate.

1 Aquella mañana Ramón (salir) de su casa a las nueve.
2 Yo (estar) en la ducha cuando (sonar) el teléfono.
3 Cuando Carmen y María (viajar) a Valencia (tener) un accidente.
4 Los niños (jugar) en el jardín cuando (empezar) a llover.
5 Juan (bajar) a pagar la cuenta, mientras yo (hacer) la maleta.
6 Mi padre siempre (sentarse) en el mismo sillón.
7 Yo (volver) a casa muy cansada.
8 (Hacer) frío cuando nosotros (llegar) a Bilbao.
9 Luis (recibir) una postal de un amigo que (vivir) en Londres.
10 El policía me (preguntar) mi nombre y dirección.

75 The two verbs 'to know'

It is important to differentiate between the verbs **saber** and **conocer**, both meaning 'to know'.

Saber is to know a fact:

No sabemos cuando llegará.   We don't know when he will arrive.
Sé que está enfermo.   I know that he is ill.

Conocer is 'to be acquainted with':

Conocemos a tu hermana muy bien.   We know your sister very well.
No conozco* esa ciudad.   I don't know that town.

*The verb **conocer** and a few others ending in **-cer** and **-cir** preceded by a vowel take a **z** before the **c** in the 1st person of the present indicative. The rest of the tense is regular.

conocer (to know)→**conozco** (I know)
obedecer (to obey)→**obedezco** (I obey)
pertenecer (to belong)→**pertenezco** (I belong)
conducir (to drive)→**conduzco** (I drive)
traducir (to translate)→**traduzco** (I translate)

76 Superlative of adjectives

The superlative is formed by putting **el más, la más, los más, las más** in front of the adjective. For example:

Este hombre es el más pobre del pueblo.   This man is the poorest in the village.
Nuestra casa es la más grande de la calle.   Our house is the biggest in the street.

When the superlative immediately follows the noun, the article is omitted:

Es el edificio más alto de Madrid.   It is the highest building in Madrid.
Es la novela más interesante que he leído.   It is the most interesting novel I have read.

77 Superlative of adverbs

The superlative is formed by putting **lo más** in front of the adverb. (**Lo** is the neuter form of the definite article.)

Hágalo Vd. lo más pronto posible.   Do it as soon as possible.
Les escribiré el martes lo más tarde.   I'll write to them on Tuesday at the latest.

78 The absolute superlative of adjectives and adverbs

The ending **-ísimo** added to adjectives or adverbs renders the English 'most', 'extremely':

Es una mujer inteligentísima.   She is a most intelligent woman.
Es un libro aburridísimo.   It is an extremely boring book.
Llegaron al aeropuerto tardísimo.   They arrived at the airport extremely late.
Hoy me he levantado tempranísimo.   Today I have got up extremely early.

Vocabulary

el disco	record
el tocadiscos	record player
el programa de televisión	television programme
divertido	amusing
la talla	size
amable	kind
interesante	interesting
la conversación	conversation
viejo	old
la farmacia	chemist's shop
la parada de autobús	bus stop

Exercise 37

Translate:

1 They don't know that record.
2 He knows that I want a record player.
3 That television programme is most amusing.
4 This size is the smallest we have.
5 These shoes are the prettiest, those are the cheapest.
6 He is the kindest man I know.
7 They don't know that I want to see them.
8 It was a most interesting conversation.
9 It is the oldest church in this town.
10 The chemist's was extremely far from the bus stop.

79 The neuter article 'lo'

We have already seen examples of **lo** preceding

a) an adverb:

Contestó lo mejor que pudo. He answered as best he could.

b) the relative **que**:

Lo que quiero decir. What I want to say.

Lo may also precede an adjective, thus making it an abstract noun:

Lo difícil es conseguir el dinero.   The difficult thing is to obtain the money.

Lo importante es llegar a tiempo.   The important thing is to arrive on time.

80 Uses of the definite and indefinite articles

The definite article is used in Spanish in the following cases

a) before nouns used in a general sense:

El vino es barato en España.   Wine is cheap in Spain.

b) before abstract nouns:

El amor es ciego.   Love is blind.

c) before titles:

La reina Isabel de Inglaterra.   Queen Elizabeth of England.

El señor y la señora Ruiz/Los señores Ruiz.   Mr. and Mrs. Ruiz.

d) before names of institutions, public places, etc:

el hospital (hospital), **la iglesia** (church), **la universidad** (university)

e) before proper nouns qualified by an adjective:

El pobre Carlos.   Poor Charles.

El viejo Madrid.   Old Madrid.

f) before parts of the body and articles of clothing, when in English the possessive adjective would be used:

Se ha roto la pierna.   He has broken his leg.

Me pondré el abrigo azul.   I shall put on my blue coat.

g) before days of the week, seasons and certain expressions of time:

Volveremos el martes.   We shall return on Tuesday.

El invierno se acerca.   Winter is approaching.

Le vi la semana pasada.   I saw him last week.

h) in certain set expressions:

El diez por ciento de rebaja.   Ten per cent reduction.
Sesenta pesetas el kilo.   Sixty pesetas per kilo.

The indefinite article *is* used before an abstract noun qualified by an adjective, for example:

Condujo a una velocidad increíble.   He drove at an incredible speed.

But it is *not* used:

a) before a noun indicating occupation, nationality, religion or politics:

Es contable.   He is an accountant.
Es española.   She is Spanish.
Soy protestante.   I am a protestant.
¿Es Vd. conservador?   Are you a conservative?

However, if the noun is qualified by an adjective the article is used:

Es un buen contable.   He is a good accountant.

b) before certain words: **otro** (another), **cierto** (certain), **medio** (half a), **cien** (a hundred), **mil** (a thousand), **tal** (such a), **¡qué!** (what a...!)

Voy a comprar otro periódico.   I am going to buy another newspaper.
Cierta mujer que conozco.   A certain woman I know.
Medio litro de leche.   Half a litre of milk.
¡Qué desastre!   What a disaster!

Vocabulary

ponerse	to put on
el guante	glove
la dependienta	shop assistant
principal	main
preocuparse	to worry
romper (se)	to break
derecho	right
el brazo	arm
hoy día	nowadays

la dificultad	difficulty
la botella	bottle
el coñac	brandy

Exercise 38

Translate:
1 Tea is a very pleasant drink.
2 Mrs. Collado will arrive on Sunday.
3 She put on her gloves because it was cold.
4 He is a waiter and she is a shop assistant.
5 I spent two weeks in hospital.
6 The main thing is not to worry.
7 Poor Mary has broken her right arm.
8 Books are very expensive nowadays.
9 He used to walk with great difficulty.
10 He is going to bring another cup.
11 We drank half a bottle of brandy.
12 The best thing is to sell the house.

Drills

16 Yo no quería invitar a Carmen ... pero tuve que invitarla.
I didn't want to invite Carmen ... but I had to invite her.

Nosotros no queríamos ir a la playa ... pero tuvimos que ir.
We didn't want to go to the beach ... but we had to go.

1 Pedro no quería escribir la carta......
2 Ellos no querían pagar la cuenta......
3 Yo no quería ver a Juan......
4 Nosotros no queríamos ir a la fiesta......
5 Vd. no quería salir del hotel......
6 Carmen no quería hacer la comida......
7 El niño no quería comer el pescado......
8 María no quería fumar un cigarrillo......
9 Yo no quería darle mi nombre......
10 Nosotros no queríamos beber la cerveza......

17 ¿Has hablado con Pedro hoy?   No, hablé ayer.
Have you spoken with Pedro today?   No, I spoke yesterday.

¿Han visto Vds. a Conchita hoy?   No, la vimos ayer.
Have you seen Conchita today?   No, we saw her yesterday.

1 ¿Han estado Vds. en la playa hoy?
2 ¿Han venido tus padres hoy?
3 ¿Ha comprado Vd. este libro hoy?
4 ¿Han pagado la cuenta hoy?
5 ¿Ha recibido Juan la postal hoy?
6 ¿Han hecho Vds. las maletas hoy?
7 ¿Ha llovido hoy?
8 ¿Han traído las flores hoy?
9 ¿Han ido Vds. al museo hoy?
10 ¿Ha visitado Vd. a sus amigos hoy?

18 Es una catedral muy grande.   It's a very large cathedral.
Sí, es la más grande que he visto.   Yes, it's the largest I've seen.

1 Es un vestido muy bonito.
2 Son unos libros muy caros.
3 Es una playa muy grande.
4 Es un hotel muy elegante.
5 Son unos programas muy divertidos.
6 Son unas ventanas muy pequeñas.

CONVERSATION

Juan y Paloma hablan de lo que han hecho durante el fin de semana
Juan and Paloma talk about what they have done during the week-end

Juan   **El sábado me levanté muy tarde porque estaba cansadísimo de trabajar tanto durante la semana.**   On Saturday I got up very late because I was exhausted after working so hard during the week.

Paloma   **¿A qué le llamas tú tarde?**   What do you call late?

Juan	**A las doce y media o la una. Era casi la hora de comer. Mi mujer no estaba muy contenta porque quería ir de compras conmigo por la mañana.** Half past twelve or one o'clock. It was almost lunch time. My wife wasn't very pleased because she wanted to go shopping with me in the morning.
Paloma	**Así que tuviste que ir por la tarde.** So you had to go in the afternoon.
Juan	**Claro. Y fue larguísimo porque las tiendas estaban llenas de gente. Así que cuando volvimos, mi mujer preparó una cena rápida y nos sentamos a ver la televisión hasta las once y media.** Of course. And it was endless, because the shops were crowded. So, when we got back, my wife prepared a quick supper and we sat down to watch television until half past eleven.
Paloma	**Yo fui a una boda el sábado. Se casaba un primo mío.** I went to a wedding on Saturday. A cousin of mine was getting married.
Juan	**¿Te divertiste?** Did you have a good time?
Paloma	**Sí, estuvo muy bien. La comida fue buenísima, y la bebida también, claro. Hubo música y baile hasta las tres de la mañana.** Yes, it was fine. The food was very good and the drink too, of course. There was music and dancing till three in the morning.
Juan	**Y el domingo ¿qué hiciste?** And Sunday, what did you do?
Paloma	**Nada importante. Dormir, leer el periódico y ver la televisión ¿Y tú?** Nothing important. Sleep, read the paper and watch television. And you?
Juan	**Poco más o menos, lo mismo que tú.** More or less the same as you.

Lesson 10

81 'Por' and 'para'

It is important to learn the uses of **por** and **para,** particularly as either word may translate the English 'for'.

Por is used to indicate means, motive, exchange. It translates the English: by, through, because of, out of, for the sake of, for:

Le di las gracias por las flores.   I thanked him for the flowers.
El ladrón entró por la ventana.   The thief came in through the window.
Lo hizo por nosotros.   He did it for us.
Envié el equipaje por tren.   I sent the luggage by train.

Para is used to indicate purpose, suitability or destination. It translates the English: for, to, in order to, so as to:

Necesito dinero para comprar los billetes.   I need money to buy the tickets.
Este abrigo es demasiado grande para mí.   This coat is too big for me.
El tren sale para Málaga dentro de cinco minutos.   The train leaves for Malaga within five minutes.
Es un regalo para Vd.   It is a present for you.

There are also many idiomatic uses of **por** and **para** which the student will learn by observation. Here are some examples:

Estamos para salir.   We are about to go out.
Estoy por no hacerlo.   I am inclined not to do it.
Lo dejaremos para mañana.   We shall leave it for tomorrow.
Una vez por semana.   Once a week.
Por la tarde.   In the afternoon (evening).
Por ejemplo.   For example.
Por último.   Finally.
Por consiguiente.   Therefore, consequently.
Por lo visto.   Evidently.

Vocabulary

joven	young
el sacrificio	sacrifice
pasar	to pass
la Aduana	Customs
cobrar	to charge
el cine	cinema
las compras	purchases, shopping
la llave	key
el armario	cupboard, wardrobe
difícil	difficult
el avión	aeroplane
cualquier cosa	anything
la curiosidad	curiosity
el melocotón	peach

Exercise 39

Fill in the gaps with 'por' or 'para' as appropriate:
1 Pagó cien mil pesetas ...... el coche.
2 No podemos salir ......esa puerta.
3 Voy de vacaciones ...... descansar.
4 Le llamaré ...... teléfono mañana.
5 Estas cartas no son ...... mí.
6 Es demasiado joven ...... comprenderlo.
7 Hizo ese sacrificio ...... su padre.
8 Hay que tener mucho dinero ...... viajar.
9 Saldremos ...... Valencia el martes.
10 No pudo venir a la fiesta ...... estar enfermo.

Exercise 40

Translate:
1 We have to pass through the Customs.
2 They charged us two thousand pesetas for the meal.
3 It is too late to go to the cinema.
4 I need a bag for all my shopping.
5 Have you (*pol.*) a key to open this cupboard?

6 This book is too difficult for him.
7 The plane leaves for Madrid at a quarter past seven.
8 I would do anything for him.
9 We read the letter out of curiosity.
10 She wants to buy some peaches for her mother.

82 The passive voice

The passive voice is formed with the verb **ser** followed by the past participle. The agent is usually introduced by **por,** although **de** is sometimes used after verbs of feeling and in some set expressions such as **cubierto de** (covered by), **acompañado de** (accompanied by). In the passive voice the past participle agrees in gender and number with the subject.

La carta fue firmada por el presidente.   The letter was signed by the president.
El soldado fue herido por una bala.   The soldier was wounded by a bullet.

Note that the past participle is also used with **estar** to indicate state, whereas with **ser** it indicates action. Compare the following examples:

El libro está publicado en cinco idiomas.   The book is published in five languages.
El libro será publicado en cinco idiomas.   The book will be published in five languages.

83 Avoidance of the passive voice

The passive voice is less frequently used in Spanish than in English, and it is often avoided by one of the following means.

a) by using the reflexive pronoun **se**:

Se prohibe fumar.   Smoking is forbidden.
El museo se cierra a las seis.   The museum is closed at six.

Se also translates the English 'one':

No se puede decir.   One cannot tell.

b) by using the 3rd person plural of the verb as an impersonal form:

Nos vieron salir de la casa.   They saw us (we were seen) leaving the house.

Dicen que no va a volver.
They say (it is said) that he is not coming back.

c) by changing the roles of subject and agent, using the active voice:

Le paró la policía.   He was stopped by the police.

Vocabulary

construir	to build
el abuelo	grandfather
acusar	to accuse
el robo	theft
el barco	boat
ahora	now
creer	to believe
muerto	dead
la montaña	mountain
cubierto	covered
la nieve	snow
la cena	dinner
servir (i)	to serve
la ventana	window
pintar	to paint
recibir	to receive
el director	director
presentar	to introduce
famoso	famous
el actor	actor

Exercise 41

Translate:
1 The house was built by his grandfather.
2 I was accused of the theft.
3 The boat was sold for eighty thousand pesetas.

4 The work is now finished.
5 It is believed that he is dead.
6 The mountains were covered in snow.
7 Dinner is not served until nine.
8 The windows were painted three weeks ago.
.9 They were received by one of the directors.
10 The programme was introduced by a famous actor.

84 Changes of spelling in verbs

Certain verbs have a change of spelling in the stem, in some parts of
the conjugation, in order to preserve the original pronunciation.
Verbs ending in:

-car change the **c** into **qu** before e:
buscar (to look for)→**busqué** (I looked for)

-zar change the **z** into **c** before e:
empezar (to begin)→**empecé** (I began)

-gar change the **g** into **gu** before e:
pagar (to pay)→**pagué** (I paid)

-ger or **-gir** change the **g** into **j** before a or o:
coger (to pick up)→**cojo** (I pick up)
dirigir (to direct)→**dirija Vd.** (direct)

An unaccented **i** between two vowels is always changed to **y**:

leer (to read)→**leyó** (he read), **leyeron** (they read)
creer (to think)→**creyó** (he thought), **creyeron** (they thought)
huir (to flee)→**huyó** (he fled), **huyeron** (they fled)
construir (to build)→**construyó** (he built), **construyeron** (they
built)
oir (to hear)→ **oyó** (he heard), **oyeron** (they heard)
caer (to fall)→**cayó** (he fell), **cayeron** (they fell)

These changes also occur in the present participle:

leyendo (reading), **creyendo** (thinking), **huyendo** (fleeing),
construyendo (building), **oyendo** (hearing), **cayendo** (falling)

Vocabulary

el aparcamiento	car park
el ruido	noise
arriba	upstairs
secar (se)	to dry (oneself)
el pie	foot
al fuego	by the fire
el suelo	ground, floor
las instrucciones	instructions
el principio	beginning
la guerra	war
el cuadro	picture
el equipaje	luggage

Exercise 42

Translate:
1 I played with the children all afternoon.
2 They are building a new car park.
3 He heard a noise upstairs.
4 I dried my feet by the fire.
5 They fell to the ground.
6 He is reading the instructions.
7 They fled from Spain at the beginning of the war.
8 I paid a lot of money for that picture.
9 Pick up the luggage, please.
10 He thought that the shop was closed.

85 Verbs followed by an infinitive

Some Spanish verbs may be directly followed by an infinitive, while others take a preposition before the infinitive. The following lists include some of the most common verbs belonging to either of these categories.

Verbs directly followed by an infinitive:

aconsejar (to advise)
Me aconsejó esperar.   He advised me to wait.

conseguir (to manage to)
Conseguimos abrirlo.   We managed to open it.

deber (must)
Debo visitarla más a menudo.   I must visit her more often.

decidir (to decide)
Decidió venir conmigo.   He decided to come with me.

esperar (to hope to)
Esperamos verle en España.   We hope to see him in Spain.

intentar (to try to)
Intenté encontrar un empleo.   I tried to find a job.

parecer (to appear to, to seem)
Pareció ser una falsa alarma.   It appeared to be a false alarm.

pedir (to ask to)
Ha pedido hablar con el gerente.   He has asked to speak to the manager.

pensar (to intend)
Pienso salir muy temprano.   I intend to leave very early.

poder (to be able to, can)
No podíamos ver nada.   We could not see anything.

Verbs followed by **a** + infinitive:

entrar (to come in)
Entró a preguntar el precio.   He came in to ask the price.

empezar (to begin)
Empezó a comer.   He began to eat.

enseñar (to teach)
Me enseño a conducir.   He taught me to drive.

aprender (to learn)
Aprendieron a nadar en seguida.   They quickly learned to swim.

decidirse (to decide)
Me decidí a decírselo.   I decided to tell him.

volver (to return)
Volvió a recoger su maleta.   He came back to collect his suitcase.

Note that **volver a** can be used idiomatically with the meaning of 'to do something again':
Volví a verle al día siguiente.   I saw him again the following day.

Verbs followed by **de** + infinitive:

acabar (to finish)
Acabó de leer la carta.   He finished reading the letter.
acabar de used in the present or imperfect indicative has the meaning of 'to have just':
Acabo de ver a Juan.   I have just seen John.
Acababan de salir.   They had just gone out.

acordarse (to remember)
No se acordó de llevar su pasaporte.   He didn't remember to take his passport.

cansarse (to get tired)
Me cansé de andar.   I got tired of walking.

dejar (to stop)
El niño dejó de llorar.   The child stopped crying.

olvidarse (to forget)
Se olvidaron de comprar gasolina.   They forgot to buy petrol.

tratar (to try)
Traté de verle.   I tried to see him.

Verbs followed by **en** + infinitive:

consentir (to consent)
Ha consentido en hablar con ella.   He has consented to speak to her.

insistir (to insist)
Insistió en acompañarme.   He insisted on accompanying me.

pensar (to think)
Pensaba en escribir a su amigo.   He was thinking of writing to his friend.

vacilar (to hesitate)
Vacilé en darle la noticia.   I hesitated to tell him the news.

tardar (to take time)
Tardó mucho en llegar.   He took a long time to arrive.

Verbs followed by **por** + infinitive:

acabar (to finish)
Acabé por darle el dinero.   I finished by giving him the money.

empezar (to begin)
Empezaremos por aprender el alfabeto.   We shall begin by learning the alphabet.

esforzarse (to make an effort)
Se esforzó por ser amable.   He made an effort to be kind.

Verbs followed by **con** + infinitive:

amenazar (to threaten)
El hombre amenazó con disparar.   The man threatened to shoot.

soñar (to dream)
Sueña con hacer mucho dinero.   He dreams of making a lot of money.

contentarse (to content oneself)
Me contento con descansar unos minutos.   I content myself with resting for a few minutes.

Vocabulary

alquilar	to hire
quejarse de	to complain
el servicio	service
jugar a	to play (a game)
el tenis	tennis
telefonear	to phone, to ring up
subir	to climb
el paquete	parcel
la discusión	argument
sonreir (i)	to smile
ganar	to earn

Exercise 43

Translate:

1 I managed to speak with them.
2 He advised us to hire a car.
3 They tried to come into the room.
4 I intend to complain about the service.
5 We are learning to play tennis.
6 I rang him up again.
7 Mr. Solís has just arrived.
8 He got tired of climbing and sat down.
9 It stopped raining and the sun came out.
10 I forgot to give him the message.
11 They insisted on paying for their tickets.
12 The parcel took two weeks to arrive.
13 They finished by having an argument.
14 The woman made an effort to smile.
15 The man threatened to call the police.
16 He contents himself with earning very little.

Drills

19 *Fill in the blanks with either 'por' or 'para' as appropriate:*

1 ¿Necesitas dinero?
  Sí, ... comprar los sellos.
2 ¿Ha comprado el vestido?
  Sí, ... cuatro mil pesetas.
3 ¿Lleva Vd. un libro?
  Sí, ... leer en la playa.
4 ¿Has comprado un regalo?
  Sí, ... mi madre.
5 ¿Ha enviado Vd. el paquete?
  Sí, ... avión.
6 ¿Salen Vds. mañana?
  Sí, ... Inglaterra.
7 ¿Necesitas gafas?
  Sí, ... leer solamente.
8 ¿Han dado Vds. un paseo?
  Sí, ... el borde del río.

20 *Avoid the passive voice by using the reflexive pronoun 'se' as in the following example:*

El piso fue vendido.   The flat was sold.
El piso se vendió.   The flat was sold.

1 El libro fue publicado.
2 Los coches fueron alquilados.
3 La puerta fue abierta.
4 Los ruidos fueron oídos.
5 El trabajo fue terminado.
6 La casa fue construida.
7 Los barcos fueron vendidos.
8 La carta fue leída.

21 ¿Has visto a mi hermano?   Have you seen my brother?
Sí, acabo de verle.   Yes, I have just seen him.

1 ¿Ha comprado Vd. los zapatos?
2 ¿Han llegado los invitados?
3 ¿Ha recibido Vd. las cartas?
4 ¿Han hecho Vds. las compras?
5 ¿Se han acostado los niños?
6 ¿Ha encontrado Vd. la llave?

CONVERSATION

Marisa y Manolo se encuentran en una cafetería
Marisa and Manolo meet in a Spanish cafeteria

Manolo **¡Por fin! Creí que no venías. Llevo aquí más de media hora.**   At last! I thought you weren't coming. I have been here more than half an hour.

Marisa **Lo siento, Manolo. Mi padre necesitaba el coche para ir a ver a unos clientes y he tenido que venir en autobús.**   I'm sorry, Manolo. My father needed the car to go and see some clients and I had to come by bus.

Manolo **Pero el autobús suele ser rápido.**   But the bus is usually quick.

Marisa **Generalmente, sí. Pero hoy hemos encontrado una manifestación en la Plaza de San Pedro y el autobús no podía pasar.**   Usually it is. But today we ran into a demonstration in St. Peter's Square and the bus could not get through.

Manolo **Y ¿para qué era la manifestación?** And what was the demonstration for?

Marisa **No sé. No he conseguido enterarme. Pero había muchos jóvenes que no dejaban de gritar y que insistían en ponerse delante del autobús.** I don't know. I didn't managed to find out. But there were many youngsters who would not stop shouting and who insisted on standing in front of the bus.

Manolo **¡Siempre hay algún jaleo! Bueno ¿qué vas a tomar?** There is always some trouble! Well, what are you going to have?

Marisa **Tengo sed. Creo que empezaré por tomar una cerveza y después, quizás, algo de comer.** I'm thirsty. I think that I'll start by having a beer and then, perhaps, something to eat.

Manolo **Yo acababa de tomar una ginebra con tónica cuando has llegado. Pero voy a tomar otra y un bocadillo de jamón porque tengo hambre.** I had just had a gin and tonic when you arrived. But I am going to have another one and a ham sandwich, because I'm hungry.

Marisa **¿Qué vamos a hacer después?** What are we going to do later?

Manolo **Pues había pensado ir al cine ¿que te parece?** Well, I thought we could go to the cinema. What do you think?

Marisa **Sí, buena idea. Hay varias películas que me gustaría ver.** Yes, good idea. There are several films that I would like to see.

Manolo **Ahora decidiremos. Primero voy a llamar al camarero.** We'll decide presently. First I am going to call the waiter.

Lesson 11

86 Uses of the verb 'deber'

Deber followed by an infinitive translates the English 'must':

Debemos salir temprano.   We must leave early.
No debes fumar tanto.   You musn't smoke so much.

Used in the conditional tense, **deber** translates 'should' and 'ought':

Vd. no debería hablar así.   You should not speak like that.
Deberíamos tener más cuidado.   We ought to be more careful.

Deber de followed by an infinitive translates 'must' (expressing assumption):

Deben de tener mucha hambre.   They must be very hungry.
El avión debe de haber llegado ya.   The plane must have arrived already.

Deber also means 'to owe':

Deben mucho dinero.   They owe a lot of money.

87 'Saber' and 'poder'

It is important not to confuse these two verbs when translating the English 'can'. Compare the following examples:

¿Sabe Vd. conducir?   Can you drive? (=Do you know how to?)
¿Puede Vd. conducir?   Can you drive? (=Are you physically able to?)

Vocabulary

la cosa   thing
las gafas   glasses

allí	there
a menudo	often
la explicación	explanation
la sortija	ring
costar (ue)	to cost
montar en bicicleta	to ride a bicycle
la píldora	pill
guisar	to cook

Exercise 44

Translate:
1 How much do I owe you (*pol.*)?
2 They ought not to say those things.
3 She must have a good job.
4 I must see a doctor.
5 Can he speak Spanish?
6 I cannot read without glasses.
7 We should go there more often.
8 He owes me an explanation.
9 That ring must cost a lot of money.
10 I cannot ride a bicycle.
11 He cannot sleep without taking pills.
12 Can you (*pol.*) cook?

88 The present subjunctive

a) Regular verbs
The present subjunctive tense of regular verbs is conjugated thus:

hablar	**comer**	**vivir**
hable	coma	viva
hables	comas	vivas
hable	coma	viva
hablemos	comamos	vivamos
habléis	comáis	viváis
hablen	coman	vivan

b) Radical-changing verbs

Radical-changing verbs of the first and second conjugations have the same stem changes as in the present indicative:

cerrar (ie)	**volver** (ue)
cierre	vuelva
cierres	vuelvas
cierre	vuelva
cerremos	volvamos
cerréis	volváis
cierren	vuelvan

Radical-changing verbs of the third conjugation have a stem change *also* in the 1st and 2nd persons plural, **e** changes to **i** and **o** changes to **u**:

pedir (i)	**sentir** (ie)	**dormir** (ue)
pida	sienta	duerma
pidas	sientas	duermas
pida	sienta	duerma
pidamos	sintamos	durmamos
pidáis	sintáis	durmáis
pidan	sientan	duerman

c) Other irregular verbs

The stem of the present subjunctive of most irregular verbs is the same as that of the 1st person singular of the present indicative. For instance:

	Present indic.	*Present subjunctive*
tener	tengo	tenga, -as, -a, etc
venir	vengo	venga, -as, -a, etc
traer	traigo	traiga, -as, -a, etc
conocer	conozco	conozca, -as, -a, etc

The exceptions to this rule are: **dar, estar, haber, ir, saber** and **ser**.

dar	**estar**	**haber**
dé	esté	haya
des	estés	hayas
dé	esté	haya
demos	estemos	hayamos
deis	estéis	hayáis
den	estén	hayan

110

ir	saber	ser
vaya	sepa	sea
vayas	sepas	seas
vaya	sepa	sea
vayamos	sepamos	seamos
vayáis	sepáis	seáis
vayan	sepan	sean

As the 1st and 3rd persons singular of the present subjunctive have the same endings, the subject pronoun is sometimes used to avoid ambiguity.

89 The perfect subjunctive

The perfect subjunctive is formed with the present subjunctive of **haber** followed by the appropriate past participle:
......**que hayan salido**...... ......that they may have gone out......
......**que hayamos visto**...... ......that we may have seen......

90 Uses of the subjunctive

The subjunctive is generally used in dependent clauses in which the action of the verb is presented not as a reality, but as a possibility, something that is yet to happen. It is used:

a) after verbs expressing wish, command, request, need, permission, prohibition, preference, doubt, emotion. For example:

Quieren que cantemos. They want us to sing.
Necesito que me ayudes. I need you to help me.
Prefiero que Vd. lo haga. I prefer you to do it.
Me prohiben que vaya. They forbid me to go.
Siento que esté Vd. enfermo. I am sorry you are ill.

Note that when the subject of the dependent verb is the same as that of the main verb, the infinitive construction is used:

Quieren cantar. They want to sing.
Prefiero hacerlo. I prefer to do it.

b) after impersonal expressions which indicate doubt, preference, possibility, probability, necessity:

Es preferible que esperemos.   It's preferable that we wait.
Es dudoso que vengan.   It's doubtful that they will come.
Es posible que lo sepa.   It's possible that he knows it.

c) after certain conjunctions when they introduce an uncertain or future action:

Se lo daré cuando le vea.   I'll give it to him when I see him.
Tendrán que pagarlo aunque no quieran.   They'll have to pay for it even if they don't want to.

d) after the following related phrases:

antes de que	before
hasta que	until
para que	so as to
sin que	without
con tal que	provided that
a no ser que	unless
después de que	after

Lo terminaré antes de que llegue.   I'll finish it before he arrives.
Saldremos sin que nos vean.   We'll go out without their seeing us.

f) after relative pronouns with indefinite negative or interrogative antecedents:

¿Hay alguien que sepa donde está?   Is there anyone who knows where it is?
No hay un hombre que no quiera triunfar.   There is not a man who doesn't want to succeed.

g) after the following expressions when they introduce a future action:

quienquiera, quienesquiera	whoever
cualquiera, cualesquiera	whatever
comoquiera	however
cuandoquiera	whenever
dondequiera	wherever

No quiero verle, quienquiera que sea.   I don't want to see him, whoever he is.

Dondequiera que vaya, siempre llevo mi pasaporte.   Wherever I go, I always carry my passport.

'However' followed by an adjective or an adverb is always rendered in Spanish by **por** + adjective/adverb + the subjunctive tense:

Por mucho que le quieras.   However much you love him.

Por caros que sean.   However expensive they may be.

Por estúpido que parezca.   However stupid it may seem.

Vocabulary

alegrarse	to be glad
el abogado	lawyer
el documento	document
mandar	to order
dudar	to doubt
sorprender	to surprise
perderse	to lose one's way
la lástima	pity
dejar	to let, to allow
el precio	price
tocar	to play (an instrument)
el piano	piano
cuidar de	to look after
el problema	problem
tener éxito	to succeed
la práctica	practice

Exercise 45

Translate:
1 I am glad they are able to come.
2 He wants the lawyer to see the documents.
3 They have ordered us to wait here.
4 I doubt that the sun will come out.
5 It surprises me that she has not written.
6 He has asked me to teach him Spanish.

7 It's possible that they have lost their way.
8 It's a pity that we haven't enough money.
9 It's probable that they will get married.
10 I won't be able to do it unless they help me.
11 We'll go to the cinema, provided you let me pay.
12 He will wait until I return.
13 They will have to eat it, even if they don't like it.
14 There is no-one who can pay that price.
15 Is there anyone who can play the piano?
16 I need a woman to look after the children.
17 We'll find it, wherever it is.
18 He will help you, whenever you have a problem.
19 However much he may try, he will never succeed.
20 However easy it may seem, one needs practice.

91 The familiar imperative

The familiar imperative corresponds to the pronouns **tú** and
vosotros, whereas the polite imperative, as we have already seen,
corresponds to **Vd.** and **Vds.**

a) Regular verbs:

hablar	habla (tú)	hablad (vosotros)	speak!
comer	come (tú)	comed (vosotros)	eat!
vivir	vive (tú)	vivid (vosotros)	live!

b) Radical-changing verbs. Only the singular form is irregular:

cerrar	cierra (tú)	cerrad (vosotros)	close!
volver	vuelve (tú)	volved (vosotros)	come back!
pedir	pide (tú)	pedid (vosotros)	ask!

c) Irregular verbs. Only the singular form is irregular:

decir	di (tú)	decid (vosotros)	say!
hacer	haz (tú)	haced (vosotros)	do!
ir	ve (tú)	id (vosotros)	go!
oír	oye (tú)	oíd (vosotros)	hear!
poner	pon (tú)	poned (vosotros)	put!
salir	sal (tú)	salid (vosotros)	go out!

ser	se (tú)	sed (vosotros)	be!
tener	ten (tú)	tened (vosotros)	have!
venir	ven (tú)	venid (vosotros)	come!

The familiar imperative only exists in the positive form; in the negative form the 2nd persons singular and plural of the present subjunctive are used.

No hables (s); **no habléis** (pl).   Don't speak.
No cierres (s); **no cerréis** (pl).   Don't close.
No vayas (s); **no vayáis** (pl).   Don't go.

Object and reflexive pronouns are attached to the end of the verb in the positive form, but they precede the verb in the negative form.

Míralo (s); **miradlo** (pl).   Look at it.
No lo mires (s); **no lo miréis** (pl).   Don't look at it.
Siéntate (s); **sentaos** (pl).   Sit down.
No te sientes (s); **no os sentéis** (pl).   Don't sit down.

Note that the final **d** of the plural form is omitted when the reflexive pronoun is attached. The exception is '**idos**' from the verb **ir**. Note also that in some cases an accent is used to preserve the original stress.

Exercise 46

Put the following verbs into the familiar imperative in both positive and negative forms, singular and plural:

1 Hacerlo.
2 Venir.
3 Acostarse.
4 Aprender.
5 Ponerlo.
6 Escribirla.
7 Gritar.
8 Oirlo.
9 Preocuparse.
10 Dormirse.

Vocabulary

enfadarse	to get angry
escuchar	to listen
vestirse (i)	to get dressed
callarse	to be quiet

despertar (ie)	to waken
perdonar	to forgive
el error	error
mover (ue)	to move

Exercise 47

Translate:
 1 Don't get angry. (*s*)
 2 Listen to me. (*pl*)
 3 Get dressed. (*s*)
 4 Don't tell me that. (*pl*)
 5 Be careful. (*pl*)
 6 Read it to us. (*s*)
 7 Be quiet. (*pl*)
 8 Don't wake me up early. (*s*)
 9 Forgive my error. (*pl*)
10 Don't move the car. (*s*)

92 Idiomatic use of 'seguir'

This verb has two meanings: 'to follow' and, with the present participle of another verb, 'to go on doing something':

El perro siguió a su amo.   The dog followed his master.
Siga Vd. trabajando.   Go on working.

'To go on doing something' can also be rendered by the verb **continuar** followed by the present participle:

La mujer continuó hablando.   The woman went on talking.

93 Idiomatic use of 'valer'

This verb can be translated by 'to cost' or 'to be worth':

¿Cuanto vale el billete?   How much does the ticket cost?
Esta pulsera no vale nada.   This bracelet is worthless.
No vale la pena.   It isn't worth it.

Valer has the same irregularities in its conjugation as **salir**.

116

Drills

22 ¿Tiene mucho dinero?　Has he a lot of money?
Sí, debe de tener mucho dinero.　Yes, he must have a lot of money.

1 ¿Está enfermo?
2 ¿Son las cinco?
3 ¿Están muy tristes?
4 ¿Trabaja mucho?
5 ¿Hace muchos años?
6 ¿Están en casa?

23 ¿Vamos a esperar?　Are we going to wait?
Sí, es preferible que esperemos.　Yes, it's better if we wait.

1 ¿Van a comer?
2 ¿Va a irse?
3 ¿Vamos a volver?
4 ¿Van a acostarse?
5 ¿Va a pagar?
6 ¿Vamos a sentarnos?

24 ¿Cierro la puerta?　Shall I shut the door?
Sí, ciérrala.　Yes, shut it.

1 ¿Pedimos los cafés?
2 ¿Traigo el vino?
3 ¿Llamamos a Miguel?
4 ¿Compro el regalo?
5 ¿Abrimos las ventanas?
6 ¿Ayudo a Pedro?

25 ¿Han terminado de hablar?　Have they finished talking?
No, siguen hablando.　No, they are still talking.

1 ¿Han terminado de comer?
2 ¿Ha terminado Juan de leer el periódico?
3 ¿Han terminado Vds. de trabajar?
4 ¿Ha terminado Vd. de pintar?
5 ¿Ha terminado Conchita de cantar?
6 ¿Han terminado de construir la casa?

CONVERSATION

La Sra. Ramos habla con su hijo Pablo, de quince años
Mrs. Ramos talks with her fifteen-year-old son, Pablo

Sra. Ramos   **Pablo, levántate que ya son las diez y media.**
Pablo, get up. It's half past ten.

Pablo   **Déjame dormir un poco más. Es sábado y no tengo
que ir al colegio.**   Let me sleep a little longer. It's
Saturday and I don't have to go to school.

Sra. Ramos   **No, pero necesito que vayas a hacerme unas
compras.**   No, but I need you to go and do some
shopping for me.

Pablo   **¿Por qué?**   Why?

Sra. Ramos   **Porque yo no tengo tiempo de salir. Vienen unos
invitados a cenar esta noche y tengo mucho que
hacer en casa,**   Because I haven't the time to go out.
I have guests coming to dinner this evening and I have
a lot to do in the house.

Pablo   **Y ¿adónde tengo que ir?**   And where do I have to
go?

Sra. Ramos   **Quiero que me traigas unas cosas del
supermercado, ahora te haré una lista, y que recojas
la carne de la carnicería.**   I want you to bring me a
few things from the supermarket – I'll make you a list
presently – and to pick up the meat from the
butcher's.

Pablo   **Espero que no me lleve mucho tiempo hacer todo
eso.**   I hope it doesn't take me long to do all that.

Sra. Ramos   **Pues, cuanto antes te levantes, antes te pondrás en
camino.**   Well, the sooner you get up the sooner
you'll be on your way.

Pablo   **¡Y yo que quería jugar al fútbol con mis amigos esta
mañana!**   And I wanted to play football with my
friends this morning!

Sra. Ramos   **¡Vamos! Date prisa y tendrás tiempo para todo. Ya
te he puesto el desayuno en la mesa.**   Come on!
Hurry up and you will have time for everything. I
have already put your breakfast on the table.

Lesson 12

94 The imperfect subjunctive

The imperfect subjunctive has two forms, with different endings.
The stem is obtained by removing the ending -ron from the 3rd
person plural of the past historic: habla-, comie-, vivie-, etc. To this
stem the following endings are added: -ra, -ras, -ra, -ramos, -rais,
-ran or -se, -ses, -se, semos, -seis, -sen.
Both forms are equally acceptable. It is very much a matter a choice
whether one or the other is used.

a) Regular verbs:

hablar	hablara, hablaras, etc
	hablase, hablases, etc
comer	comiera, comieras, etc
	comiese, comieses, etc
vivir	viviera, vivieras, etc
	viviese, vivieses, etc

b) Radical-changing verbs:

cerrar	cerrara, cerraras, etc
	cerrase, cerrases, etc
volver	volviera, volvieras, etc
	volviese, volvieses, etc
pedir	pidiera, pidieras, etc
	pidiese, pidieses, etc

c) Irregular verbs:

estar	estuviera, estuvieras, etc
	estuviese, estuvieses, etc
tener	tuviera, tuvieras, etc
	tuviese, tuvieses, etc
decir	dijera, dijeras, etc
	dijese, dijeses, etc

95 Pluperfect subjunctive

This tense is formed with the imperfect subjunctive of **haber** followed by the past participle of the appropriate verb:

Hubiera (hubiese) visto.   He might have seen.
Hubieramos (hubiésemos) vendido.   We might have sold.

96 Uses of the imperfect and pluperfect subjunctive

These tenses are used under the same conditions as the present and perfect subjunctive, but they generally follow a different tense in the main clause. Coompare the following examples:

Quiere que lo compres.   He wants you to buy it.
Quería que lo compraras.   He wanted you to buy it.
Espero que haya llegado.   I hope he has arrived.
Esperaba que hubiera llegado.   I hoped he had arrived.
Me dice que le escriba.   He tells me to write to him.
Me dijo que le escribiera.   He told me to write to him.
Es importante que lo haga.   It's important that he does it.
Era importante que lo hiciese.   It was important that he did it.

97 Sequence of tenses

The present and perfect subjunctive usually follow the present indicative, the future, the imperative and the perfect.

The imperfect and pluperfect subjunctive usually follow the imperfect indicative, the past historic, the conditional and the pluperfect.

Occasionally the imperfect and pluperfect subjunctive may follow a verb in the present indicative:

Siento mucho que no pudiera venir.   I'm very sorry he could not come.
No es posible que lo supieran.   It's not possible that they knew.
No creo que nos hubieran invitado.   I don't think they would have invited us.

Vocabulary

viajar	to travel
el accidente	accident
poner la mesa	to lay the table
darse prisa	to hurry
esperar	to hope
avisar	to warn
usar	to use
la máquina	machine
reservar	to book
la persona	person
traducir	to translate
ganar	to win
el premio	prize

Exercise 48

Translate:
1 They wanted me to travel with them.
2 I was afraid that he might have had an accident.
3 She told us to lay the table.
4 I asked him to hurry up.
5 We hoped that it would not be too hot in Seville.
6 Wherever he went, he always found friends.
7 I warned him not to use that machine.
8 He phoned me so that I would book the rooms.
9 They were looking for a person who could translate the letter.
10 I am glad that they won the first prize.

98 The subjunctive in conditional sentences

The subjunctive is used in an 'if' clause when the action of the verb is uncertain or hypothetical:

Lo compraría si tuviese el dinero.   I would buy it if I had the money.
Acabaríamos antes si me ayudaras.   We would finish sooner if you helped me.

When the action of the verb can be fulfilled, the indicative is used:

Lo compraré si tengo el dinero.   I'll buy it if I have the money.
Acabaremos antes si me ayudas.   We'll finish sooner if you help me.

When the tense of the main verb is a conditional perfect, it is usually replaced by the **-ra** form of the pluperfect subjunctive:

No le hubiera insultado si no me hubiese provocado.   I would not have insulted him if he had not provoked me.

The future and conditional tenses are not used with **si** except when it means 'whether':

No sé si vendrá.   I don't know whether he will come.
No me dijo si lo vendería.   He didn't tell me whether he would sell it.

Vocabulary

el perro	dog
morder (ue)	to bite
pegar	to hit
guardar	to keep
el bolsillo	pocket
divertirse (ie)	to have a good time
quedarse	to stay
más tiempo	longer
el paraguas	umbrella
mojarse	to get wet
el concierto	concert

Exercise 49

Translate:
1 I would do it, if I could.
2 If the weather is fine, I'll work in the garden.
3 The dog would not have bitten you, if you had not hit it.
4 If you asked them, they wouldn't know what to say.
5 If I saw him now, I would not speak to him.
6 You (*polite*) would not have lost the money, if you had kept it in your pocket.
7 If they came to the party, they would have a good time.

8 I shall write to you, if I have to stay there longer.
9 If you don't take an umbrella, you'll get wet.
10 I would go to the concert, if he'd come with me.

99 The subjunctive in main clauses

The subjunctive is used . . .

a) in all imperatives, except the positive form of the familiar imperative:

Hable Vd., hablen Vds.   Speak (*polite*).
No hable Vd., no hablen Vds., no hables, no habléis.   Don't speak (*polite and familiar*).
but: **Habla, hablad**   Speak (*familiar*).

b) to express a wish:

¡Que tenga Vd. buen viaje!   Have a good journey!
¡Que se mejore Vd.!   Get well soon!
¡Que sean muy felices!   May they be very happy!

c) after the word **ojalá** ('if only', 'would that. . .'):

¡Ojalá pudiera verle!   If only I could see him!
¡Ojalá ganáramos las quinielas!   Would that we won the pools!

d) after **quizá (s), tal vez, acaso** ('perhaps'). Sometimes the indicative is used, depending on the degree of doubt:

Quizá no venga hoy.   Perhaps he won't come today.
Acaso no lo sepan.   Perhaps they don't know it.
Tal vez no habían oído la noticia.   Perhaps they hadn't heard the news.

e) in certain set expressions:

Sea como sea.   Be that as it may.
Sea lo que sea.   Whatever it is.
Pase lo que pase.   Whatever happens.
Diga lo que diga.   Whatever he says.
Hagan lo que hagan.   Whatever they do.

f) to translate the English 'let':

Que espere.   Let him wait.
Que paguen.   Let them pay.

100 'May' and 'might'

When they indicate possibility, 'may' and 'might' can be translated by any of the following expressions:

puede que, es posible que, quizá(s), tal vez: may
pudiera, era posible que, quizá(s), tal vez: might

Puede que estén trabajando.   They may be working.
Es posible que llueva.   It may rain.
Pensó que pudiera haber ocurrido.   He thought that it might have happened.
Dijo que era posible que volvieran.   He said that they might return.

When 'may' and 'might' are used to express permission, they are translated by the present or imperfect indicative:

¿Puedo entrar?   May I come in?
Dijeron que podíamos jugar con ellos.   They said we might play with them.

Vocabulary

perder	to miss (a train, boat, etc)
estar en contacto con	to be in touch
la fotografía	photograph
el día libre	day off
el aviso	warning (sign)

Exercise 50

Translate:
1 If only I did not have to work.
2 Perhaps he is ill.

3 We may have missed the train.
4 Let him come, if he likes.
5 If only we could have a holiday.
6 Whatever happens, I'll be in touch with you (*pol.*).
7 May we see the photographs?
8 He said that I might have the day off.
9 Have a good time! (*pol.*)
10 Perhaps they did not see the warning sign.

101 Verbs followed by prepositions

We have already seen some common verbs that take a preposition before an infinitive (see section 85). Here now are some verbs that take a prepositional object.

acercarse a (to approach, to go near)
El hombre se acercó a la casa.   The man approached the house.
asomarse a (to lean out of)
La niña se asomó a la ventana.   The girl leaned out of the window.
casarse con (to marry)
Por fin no se casó con ella.   In the end he did not marry her.
contar con (to count on, to rely on)
No puedo contar con mi hermano.   I cannot rely on my brother.
dar a (to overlook)
Los balcones daban al mar.   The balconies overlooked the sea.
depender de (to depend on)
El resultado no depende de mí.   The result does not depend on me.
despedirse de (to say good-bye to)
Vinieron a despedirse de nosotros.   They came to say good-bye to us.
dudar de (to doubt)
No dude Vd. de su palabra.   Do not doubt his word.
enamorarse de (to fall in love with)
Se enamoró de una chica muy joven.   He fell in love with a very young girl.
encontrarse con (to meet, to come across)
Me encontré con un viejo amigo.   I came across an old friend.
enterarse de (to find out, to hear about)
No me había enterado de su muerte.   I had not heard about his death.

fijarse en (to notice)
¿Se ha fijado Vd. en el sombrero de Anita?   Have you noticed
Anita's hat?
ocuparse de (to attend to)
Nos ocuparemos de los invitados.   We'll attend to the guests.
parecerse a (to resemble, to look like)
No se parece a su padre.   He doesn't look like his father.
pensar en (to think of)
Siempre está pensando en sus hijos.   He is always thinking of his
children.
pensar de (to think of, to have an opinion on)
¿Qué piensa Vd. de esa película?   What do you think of that film?
saber a (to taste of)
Este pastel sabe a canela.   This cake tastes of cinnamon.
soñar con (to dream of)
Anoche soñé contigo.   Last night I dreamt of you.

Vocabulary

el borde	edge
la ventanilla	window (of a vehicle)
concurrido (-a)	busy, crowded
el éxito	success
la obra (de teatro)	play
el compañero	colleague, companion
la buena intención	good will
tonto (-a)	silly
fácil	easy
el/la turista	tourist
el nombre	name
la situación	situation
el helado	ice cream
la fresa	strawberry
el lugar	place

Exercise 51

Translate:
  1 Don't go near the edge.
  2 He leaned out of the car window.

3 My brother is going to marry an English girl.
4 You know that you can count on me.
5 The window overlooked a very busy street.
6 The success of the play depends on the actors.
7 I have to say good-bye to my colleagues.
8 They don't doubt his good will.
9 Maria has fallen in love with a very silly man.
10 It's very easy to meet English tourists in Spain.
11 We have not been able to find out his name.
12 I didn't notice what she was wearing.
13 You have to attend to the drinks.
14 This house looks very much like ours.
15 He doesn't want to think of all the problems.
16 We don't know what he thinks of the situation.
17 This ice cream tastes of strawberry.
18 I was dreaming of all the places I had visited.

102 'Al' followed by infinitive

This is a very common construction in Spanish. It translates the English 'on' + present participle:

Le vi al salir del hotel. I saw him on leaving the hotel.
Al entrar en el cuarto todo el mundo dejó de hablar. On entering the room everybody stopped talking.

It may also translate sentences with 'when' and 'as':

Sonrió al verme. He smiled when he saw me.
Le saludé con la mano al entrar. I waved at him as I came in.

Drills

26 ¿Va a venir? Is he going to come?
   Puede que venga. He may come.
 1 ¿Va Vd. a venderlo?
 2 ¿Van a casarse?
 3 ¿Van Vds. a salir?
 4 ¿Va a volver?
 5 ¿Van a invitarnos?
 6 ¿Va Vd. a nadar?

27 *Change the verb in the future into the conditional, followed by the appropriate form of the subjunctive. Thus:*
Lo compraré si tengo dinero.   I'll buy it if I have money.
Lo compraría si tuviera dinero.   I'd buy it if I had the money.

1 Vendrán si pueden.
2 Lo pediremos si lo necesitamos.
3 Comeré si tengo hambre.
4 Se lo diremos si le vemos.
5 Saldrán si no llueve.
6 Te lo daré si lo encuentro.
7 Trabajará más si le pagan bien.
8 Hablaré con ellos si vienen.

28 Se pararon cuando llegaron al puente.
They stopped when they arrived at the bridge.

Se pararon al llegar al puente.
They stopped on arriving at the bridge.

1 Se sorprendió cuando oyó la noticia.
2 Gritaron cuando vieron a los policías.
3 Lloraba cuando leía la carta.
4 Me pidió la llave cuando salía.
5 Tuve miedo cuando oí un ruido.
6 Se lavaron las manos cuando terminaron.
7 Me quité el sombrero cuando entré.
8 Empezó a llover cuando llegamos a casa.

CONVERSATION

Una invitación a cenar
An invitation to dinner
El teléfono suena.   The phone rings.

Alfonso   **¡Dígame!**   Hello!
Pilar   **¿Eres Alfonso?**   Is that Alfonso?
Alfonso   **Sí. ¿Quién es?**   Yes. Who is it?
Pilar   **Soy Pilar.**   It's Pilar.
Alfonso   **¡Hola Pilar! No te había conocido. ¿Cómo estás?**
Hello Pilar! I didn't recognise your voice. How are you?

Pilar   **Muy bien. ¿Y tú?**   Very well. And you?

Alfonso   **Bien, gracias. ¿ Querías hablar con Conchita? Ha ido a recoger a los niños al colegio.**   Fine, thanks. Did you want to speak to Conchita? She has gone to collect the children from school.

Pilar   **¡Ah! Bueno, no importa. La razón por la que llamo es para ver si tú y Conchita queréis venir a cenar el viernes.**   Oh! Well, it doesn't matter. The reason I'm ringing is to see if you and Conchita would like to come to dinner on Friday.

Alfonso   **El viernes no podemos porque llega mi madre de Barcelona a pasar unos días con nosotros, y tenemos que ir al aeropuerto a las nueve de la noche. Lo siento mucho, Pilar.**   We can't on Friday, because my mother is coming from Barcelona to spend a few days with us, and we have to go to the airport at nine o'clock in the evening. I'm sorry, Pilar.

Pilar   **No te preocupes. ¿Podéis venir el sábado?**   Don't worry. Can you come on Saturday?

Alfonso   **El sábado, sí. Lo único es que no me gustaría dejar sola a mi madre.**   On Saturday, yes. The only thing is I would not like to leave my mother alone.

Pilar   **Pues, que venga también. Encantada de tener una invitada más.**   Well, let her come too. Delighted to have one more guest.

Alfonso   **En ese caso, estupendo. ¿A qué hora nos esperas?**   In that case, fine. What time do you expect us?

Pilar   **¿Te parece bien a las ocho? Así tenemos tiempo de tomar un aperitivo antes de cenar.**   Is eight o'clock all right for you? That way we'll have time to have a drink before dinner.

Alfonso   **Muy bien. Se lo diré a Conchita. Hasta el sábado y gracias.**   Very well. I'll tell Conchita. Till Saturday and thank you.

Pilar   **De nada. Adiós.**   Not at all. 'Bye.

Lesson 13

103 Some important verbs

It is important that you should learn not only the meaning of the following verbs, but also how to use them in different contexts.

asistir (to assist, to attend)
Tuve que asistir al herido.   I had to assist the injured man.
Asistimos a una representación de Aida.   We attended a performance of Aida.

bastar (to be enough, to suffice)
No basta decírselo.   It's not enough to tell him.
Este pan nos basta para el desayuno.   This bread is enough for our breakfast.

caber (to fit in)
No cabemos todos en un coche.   We don't all fit into one car.
Este armario no cabe en esa habitación.   This wardrobe does not fit into that room.

devolver (to return, to give back)
Me ha devuelto mi carta.   He has returned my letter.
Nos devolvieron el dinero.   They refunded our money.

echar (to throw, to pour)
Eché la carta al fuego.   I threw the letter on the fire.
Echó el té en la taza.   She poured the tea in the cup.

faltar (to lack, to be missing)
No le falta inteligencia.   He doesn't lack intelligence.
Faltan dos páginas en este libro.   There are two pages missing in this book.

hacer falta (to need)
No hace falta ir más lejos.   There is no need to go any further.
Me hace falta más gasolina.   I need more petrol.

meter (to put in, to insert)
Metió la llave en la cerradura.   He put the key in the lock.

Me metí la mano en el bolsillo.   I put my hand in my pocket.

quedar (to remain, to have left)
Quedan cuatro lecciones.   There remain four lessons.
Me quedan cuarenta libras.   I have forty pounds left.

quitar(se) (to take away, to take off)
Le quitaron el pasaporte.   They took his passport.
Me quité los zapatos.   I took off my shoes.

sobrar (to have more than enough, to have to spare)
Sobran candidatos para ese trabajo.   There are more than enough candidates for that job.
¿Te sobra algo de dinero?   Have you any money to spare?

tocar (to touch, to play an instrument)
No toque Vd. la pintura.   Don't touch the paint.
Toca la guitarra maravillosamente.   He plays the guitar beautifully.

tomar (to take, to have food or dink)
Tomó al niño en sus brazos.   He took the child in his arms.
Vamos a tomar un café.   Let's have a coffee.

Vocabulary

la gente	people
el entierro	funeral
la cantidad	amount
la harina	flour
la caja	box
el maletero	car boot
prestar	to lend
la pelota	ball
el estante	shelf
el ayudante	helper
la silla	chair
la chaqueta	jacket
el huevo	egg
la tortilla	omelet
la seda	silk
el violín	violin
firmar	to sign

Exercise 52

Translate:

1 Many people attended the funeral.
2 This amount of flour will be enough.
3 That box doesn't fit in the boot of the car.
4 I want to return the magazine he lent me.
5 He threw the ball to the children.
6 I am going to pour the wine.
7 They lack experience.
8 There are five books missing from this shelf.
9 We need more helpers.
10 They will put all the clothes in one suitcase.
11 How many days have you left?
12 He will take away these chairs.
13 May I take off my jacket?
14 There are more than enough eggs to make the omelet.
15 It's very pleasant to touch silk.
16 He would like to play the violin.
17 He took the pen and signed the letter.
18 They like to have wine with their meal.

104 'Más' and 'menos'

We have already seen these two words in the comparatives **más que** (more than) and **menos que** (less than). But when 'more than' and 'less than' are followed by a numeral, they are translated by **más de** and **menos de**. For example:

Hay más de quinientos alumnos en esa escuela. There are more than five hundred pupils in that school.
He pagado menos de trescientas pesetas. I have paid less than three hundred pesetas.

In the negative, **que** replaces **de** and **no. . .más que** is translated by 'only':

No tengo más que un hermano. I have only one brother.
No hay más que tres manzanas. There are only three apples.

When **más de** and **menos de** are followed by a clause, the forms **el**

que, la que, los que, las que must be used. If no definite noun is referred to, **lo que** is used. Thus:

Tenemos más comida de la que necesitamos.   We have more food than we need.
Es más inteligente de lo que parece.   He is more intelligent than he looks.

105 'Tan' and 'tal'

Both words translate the English 'such', but **tan** precedes an adjective whereas **tal(es)** precedes a noun:

Es un libro tan interesante.   It's such an interesting book.
No conozco a tal hombre.   I don't know such a man.

Tan is also used in exclamations:

¡Qué casa tan bonita!   What a lovely house!
¡Qué día tan horrible!   What a horrible day!

The adjective **semejante** can also translate 'such':

No diga Vd. semejante cosa.   Don't say such a thing.

106 'Pero' and 'sino'

Although 'but' is generally translated by **pero,** remember to use **sino** after a negative statement when 'but' introduces a clause that is contrary to the first statement:

Este regalo no es para mi madre, sino para mi hermana. This present is not for my mother, but for my sister.
No he pedido carne, sino pescado.   I haven't ordered meat, but fish.

Vocabulary

heredar   to inherit
el collar   necklace

feo	ugly
el edificio	building
aburrido	boring
listo	clever

Exercise 53

Translate:
1 He has inherited more than twenty million pesetas.
2 I cannot sell it for less than ten thousand pesetas.
3 We have lived in Madrid more than fifteen years.
4 I shall do it in less than five minutes.
5 He had never seen such a beautiful necklace.
6 What an ugly building!
7 He wouldn't do such a thing.
8 I find such books very boring.
9 That is not my brother, but my cousin.
10 They don't have a dog, but they have two cats.
11 He has more money than he says.
12 They are cleverer than you think.
13 What a good idea!
14 It is such a long journey!

107 Prepositions

Here is a list of the most common simple and compound prepositions. **Por** and **para** are not included, as they have been dealt with in lesson 10.

a (to, at)   Used in expressions of time and a few set phrases such as: **a la mesa** 'at table', **a la puerta** 'at the door'.
Van a la playa.   They go to the beach.
Te veré a las ocho.   I'll see you at eight.
Nos sentamos a la mesa.   We sat at the table.

ante (before) When meaning 'in the presence of', 'faced with'.
Ante ese problema, no supo que hacer.   Faced with that problem, he didn't know what to do.
Se presentó ante el tribunal.   He appeared before the court.

antes de (before time)
Llegaremos antes de las cuatro.   We shall arrive before four
o'clock.

bajo (under)
Trabaja bajo su dirección.   He works under him.

debajo de (under = underneath)
Encontré la sortija debajo del sillón.   I found the ring under the
armchair.

con (with)
Iremos con Juan.   We'll go with John.
¿Quiere Vd. venir conmigo?   Do you want to come with me?

contra (against)
Ponga Vd. esa silla contra la pared.   Put that chair against the
wall.

de (of, from, about)
La casa de Conchita.   Conchita's house.
Estamos hablando de Vd.   We are talking about you.
Trabajo de nueve a dos.   I work from nine till two.

delante de (in front of)
Andaba delante de mí.   He was walking in front of me.

desde (from) This is more emphatic than **de**.
Desde la ventana se ve el mar.   From the window one can see the
sea.

después de (after = time)
Después de cenar daremos un paseo.   After dinner we shall go for
a walk.

detrás de (behind)
El garaje está detrás de la casa.   The garage is behind the house.

en (in, on, at)
El regalo está en la caja.   The present is in the box.
La comida está en la mesa.   The food is on the table.
Estarán en casa todo el día.   They will be at home all day.

encima de (on top of, over)
La maleta está encima del armario.   The suitcase is on top of the
wardrobe.

enfrente de (opposite)
La farmacia esta enfrente del banco.   The chemist's is opposite the bank.

entre (between)
Podemos pagar los gastos entre nosotros.   We can pay the expenses between us.

hacia (towards, about = of time)
El niño vino hacia nosotros.   The boy came towards us.
Volveremos hacia el veinte de septiembre.   We shall come back towards the 20th of September.

hasta (until, as far as)
Durmió hasta las once.   He slept until eleven.
Me acompañó hasta la parada de autobús.   He accompanied me as far as the bus stop.

según (according to)
Según el hombre del tiempo, va a llover.   According to the weather man, it's going to rain.

sin (without)
No podemos viajar sin pasaporte.   We cannot travel without a passport.

sobre (on, upon, about)
Las cartas están sobre la mesa.   The letters are on the table.
Tenemos que hablar sobre ese tema.   We have to talk about that subject.

tras (after)
El perro corrió tras la pelota.   The dog ran after the ball.

Vocabulary

espléndido	generous
la fila	line, row
el juez	judge
la cama	bed
la zapatería	shoe shop
la panadería	bakery
el piso	floor

probar	to try, to test
el sofá	sofa
el paquete	parcel
el escritorio	desk

Exercise 54

Translate:

1 The man was sleeping under a tree.
2 He wrote to me from Cordoba.
3 After the theatre, we went to his house.
4 He is very generous with his friends.
5 We waited at the door, but he did not come.
6 According to his father, he is very ill.
7 There was a long line of cars in front of me.
8 He had to appear before the judge.
9 They left without paying for the drink.
10 He put the suitcase under the bed.
11 There is a shoe shop opposite the bakery.
12 I won't see you until Sunday.
13 The lift stopped between the two floors.
14 I want to try it before buying it.
15 We shall start walking towards the station.
16 They will have to go on the bus.
17 The book has fallen behind the sofa.
18 I shall leave the parcel on top of the desk.

108 Augmentatives and diminutives

Certain augmentative and diminutive endings are added to nouns, to qualify their meaning. As the use of these terminations can present considerable difficulties, without a thorough knowledge of the language, the student is advised to employ adjectives instead.

a) Augmentatives:

-ón, -azo, -acho, -ote express largeness and may also imply some degree of awkwardness or ugliness.

un hombrón   a big man
unos ojazos   big eyes
una mujerona   a big woman

b) Diminutives:

-ito, -ico, -illo, -uelo express smallness and sometimes fondness on
the part of the speaker.

un perrito   a little dog
un corrillo   a small circle of people
un polluelo   a chick

Many augmentatives and diminutives have established themselves as
words in their own right:

ventana (window)→**ventanilla** (window of a vehicle)
silla (chair)→**sillín** (saddle), **sillón** (arm-chair)
puerta (door)→**portezuela** (door of a vehicle)
cera (wax)→**cerillas** (matches)
caja (box)→**cajón** (drawer)
camisa (shirt)→**camisón** (night dress)
pan (bread)→**panecillo** (roll)
niebla (fog)→**neblina** (mist)

Drills

29 ¿Necesita Vd. el paraguas? Do you need the umbrella?
No, no me hace falta. No, I don't need it.

¿Necesitan Vds. sellos? Do you need stamps?
No, nos hacen falta. No, we don't need them.

1 ¿Necesita Carmen el coche?
2 ¿Necesitan Vds. el pasaporte?
3 ¿Necesita Vd. estas cajas?
4 ¿Necesitan ellos ayuda?
5 ¿Necesita Ramón las gafas?
6 ¿Necesitan Vds. otra maleta?

30 Ha firmado Vd. la carta? Have you signed the letter?
No puedo firmarla todavía. I cannot sign it yet.

1 ¿Han devuelto Vds. el dinero?
2 ¿Ha metido Vd. la ropa en la maleta?
3 ¿Han echado ellos las postales?
4 ¿Se ha quitado Vd. los zapatos?
5 ¿Han tomado Vds. vino?
6 ¿Ha pagado Carlos la cuenta?

31 *Fill in the blanks with the appropriate preposition from the column on the right*

1 Trabajaré ...... las cinco.	en
2 Nos escribirá ...... Sevilla.	sin
3 El hotel está ...... la playa.	hacia
4 He dejado la maleta ...... la cama.	antes de
5 ...... los dos podemos mover el armario.	enfrente de
6 No puedes salir ......abrigo.	desde
7 Queremos hablar ...... el gerente.	encima de
8 No podré llegar ...... las diez.	con
9 Te esperaremos ...... casa.	entre
10 Los niños corrieron ...... su padre.	hasta

CONVERSATION

En el tren
On the train

Felipe **¿Perdone, está ocupado este asiento?** Excuse me. Is this seat taken?

Lolita **No, no creo.** No, I don't think so.

Felipe **Menos mal. Creí que no iba a encontrar sitio. El tren está casi lleno.** Thank goodness. I thought I wasn't going to find a place. The train is almost full.

Lolita **Es verdad. Nunca he visto tanta gente en este tren.** It's true. I have never seen so many people on this train.

Felipe **¿Le importa que abra un poco la ventanilla? Tengo mucho calor.** Do you mind if I open the window a little? I am very hot.

Lolita **Abrala. Yo también necesito un poco de aire fresco.** Open it. I too need a little fresh air.

Felipe	**¿Quiere Vd. un pitillo?**	Would you like a cigarette?
Lolita	**No, gracias. No fumo.**	No thanks. I don't smoke.
Felipe	**¿Le molesta que fume yo?**	Do you mind if I smoke?

Lolita **En absoluto. Aunque no fumo, me gusta el olor del tabaco.** Not at all. Although I don't smoke, I like the smell of tobacco.

Felipe **¿No ha fumado Vd. nunca?** Have you never smoked?

Lolita **Sí, pero lo dejé hace dos años.** Yes, but I gave it up two years ago.

Felipe **Yo llevo mucho tiempo tratando de dejarlo, pero no lo consigo. Me falta fuerza de voluntad.** I have been trying a long time to give it up, but I am not succeeding. I lack will-power.

Lolita **Bueno, parece que nos ponemos en marcha. ¿Va Vd. a Segovia?** Well, it looks as if we are moving. Are you going to Segovia?

Felipe **Sí. Tengo que visitar una fábrica allí. No voy a estar más que dos días. Y ¿Vd.?** Yes. I have to visit a factory there. I am only going to stay a couple of days. And you?

Lolita **Yo también voy a Segovia, a pasar una semana con unos amigos. ¡Ay, qué rabia! He olvidado comprar algo para leer en el viaje.** I am going to Segovia too, to spend a week with some friends. Oh, bother! I have forgotten to buy something to read on the journey.

Felipe **¿Quiere Vd. esta revista?** Would you like this magazine?

Lolita **Si a Vd. no le hace falta de momento, me gustaría verla. Gracias.** If you don't need it for the moment, I'd like to see it. Thanks.

Reading practice

The following extracts from works by modern Spanish authors each have an English translation on the facing page. Refer to this as little as possible during your first reading of the Spanish, then go through the piece again, noting constructions and vocabulary.

Los Españolitos de Alsemberg

A Santi se le hizo muy cuesta arriba vivir en la casa de los Dufour. Y no es que no le tratasen bien, no. Al contrario, tanto Raymond Dufour como su mujer, Arlette, hicieron desde el principio todo lo posible para que Santi se sintiese a sus anchas y para que no le faltase nada de cuanto podía necesitar o desear.

Durante varios días, Arlette y Raymond Dufour habían estado hablando de como sería el niño español que había de venir a su casa y era cosa decidida que ellos harían todo lo posible para tratarle con comprensión y cariño. Vivían en una casa amplia, muy bonita, de dos pisos, como un chalet, en el barrio de Forest, cerca de un parque lleno de flores y de campos de tenis y de fútbol, con pequeños tio-vivos y toboganes y columpios. Era un parque alegre y sonriente que estaba todo el día lleno de niños, de escolares, de niñeras y de palomas. Para Santi habían hecho empapelar y amueblar especialmente una habitación muy simpática, luminosa, con una pequeña chimenea, estanterías llenas de libros españoles y muchas pinturas y fotografías de España y banderines y juguetes.

Pero nada más entrar en la habitación, aquella primera noche, Santi supo que no se iba a encontrar a gusto. Se sintió emocionado al observar el cariño con que los Dufour habían preparado todo aquello para él y captó la mirada expectante de Madame Dufour que parecía preguntarse, con angustia, si aquello le gustaba o no.

Santi era cortés y tenía un gran sentido de gratitud. Dijo que todo era muy bonito y que gracias. Madame Dufour le abrazó y habló con su marido y Raymond Dufour dijo:

–Dice que quiere que seas feliz con nosotros, Santiago.

Ella le trajo un vaso de leche y unas galletas y aunque Santi no tenía ninguna gana de tomar nada, tomó el vaso de leche por complacerla. Las galletas no, porque realmente no podía.

La cama era cómoda y limpia. Raymond Dufour había depositado la maleta de Santi al lado de la cama y Santi no sabía qué hacer. Bostezó dos veces adrede – aunque estaba realmente muy cansado; las emociones del día le habían agotado – y Madame Dufour pronunció unas palabras en francés. Monsieur Dufour dijo:

–Duerme bien, Santiago. Mañana iremos de compras y también iremos en coche de paseo por Bruselas para que veas la ciudad. Luego almorzaremos en un restaurante, compras el regalo que quieras para tu hermana, e iremos a verla. ¿Te parece?

The Spanish Children of Alsemberg

Santi found it very hard to live in the Dufour's house. It wasn't that they did not treat him well. On the contrary, from the beginning both Raymond Dufour and his wife Arlette did all they could to make Santi feel at ease and to give him everything that he needed or wished.

For several days, Arlette and Raymond Dufour had been talking of what the little Spanish boy who was coming to their house might be like, and they decided that they would do everything in their power to treat him with understanding and love. They lived in a big, two-storey house, very pretty, like a villa, in the Forest district, near a park full of flowers, with tennis courts and a football pitch, with small roundabouts and slides and swings. It was a cheerful, jolly park which was always full of children, school boys, nannies and pigeons. They had had a room papered and furnished specially for Santi, a very pleasant, light room, with a small fireplace, book shelves full of Spanish books and many pictures and photographs of Spain and pennants and toys.

But as soon as Santi entered the room, that first night, he knew that he wasn't going to feel happy there. He was touched by the love with which the Dufours had prepared all that for him and he was aware of the expectant look of Madame Dufour, who seemed to be wondering, anxiously, whether he liked all that or not.

Santi was polite and he had a great sense of gratitude. He said that everything was very nice and he thanked them. Madame Dufour hugged him and spoke to her husband and Raymond Dufour said: 'She says that she wants you to be happy with us, Santiago'.

She brought him a glass of milk and some biscuits and although Santi didn't feel like having anything, he drank the milk just to please her. He didn't eat the biscuits, he really couldn't.

The bed was comfortable and clean. Raymond Dufour had left Santi's suitcase by the bed and Santi didn't know what to do next. He yawned twice on purpose – although he really was very tired; the emotions of the day had made him feel exhausted – and Madame Dufour said a few words in French. Monsieur Dufour said: 'Sleep well, Santiago. Tomorrow we shall go shopping and we shall also go for a ride in the car round Brussels so that you can see the city. Then we shall have lunch in a restaurant, you buy any present you like for your sister and we shall go to visit her. Does that suit you?'

Primera Memoria

– Te domaremos – me dijo mi abuela, apenas llegué a la isla.

Tenía doce años, y por primera vez comprendí que me quedaría allí para siempre. Mi madre murió cuatro años atrás y Mauricia – la vieja aya que me cuidaba – estaba impedida por una enfermedad. Mi abuela se hacía cargo definitivamente de mí, estaba visto.

El día que llegué a la isla, hacía mucho viento en la ciudad. Unos rótulos medio desprendidos tableteaban sobre las puertas de las tiendas. Me llevó la abuela a un hotel oscuro, que olía a humedad y lejía. Mi habitación daba a un pequeño patio, por un lado, y, por el otro, a un callejón, tras cuya embocadura se divisaba un paseo donde se mecían las palmeras sobre un pedazo de mar plomizo. La cama de hierro forjado, muy complicada, me amedrentó como un animal desconocido. La abuela dormía en la habitación contigua, y de madrugada me desperté sobresaltada – como me ocurría a menudo – y busqué, tanteando, con el brazo extendido, el interruptor de la luz de la mesilla. Recuerdo bien el frío de la pared estucada, y la pantalla rosa de la lámpara. Me estuve muy quieta, sentada en la cama, mirando recelosa alrededor, asombrada del retorcido mechón de mi propio cabello que resaltaba oscuramente contra mi hombro. Habituándome a la penumbra, localicé, uno a uno, los desconchados de la pared, las grandes manchas del techo, y sobre todo, las sombras enzarzadas de la cama, como serpientes, dragones, o misteriosas figuras que apenas me atrevía a mirar. Incliné el cuerpo cuanto pude hacia la mesilla, para coger el vaso de agua, y entonces, en el vértice de la pared, descubrí una hilera de hormigas que trepaba por el muro. Solté el vaso, que se rompió al caer, y me hundí de nuevo entre las sábanas, tapándome la cabeza. No me decidía a sacar ni una mano, y así estuve mucho rato, mordiéndome los labios y tratando de ahuyentar las despreciables lágrimas. Me parece que tuve miedo. Acaso pensé que estaba completamente sola, y, como buscando algo que no sabía.

Taken from the novel 'Primera Memoria' by Ana Maria Matute (born 1926).

← 'Los Españolitos de Alsemberg' is taken from 'El otro árbol de Guernica' (The other tree of Guernica) by Luis de Castresana (born 1925).

First Memory

'We shall tame you' my grandmother told me as soon as I arrived on the island.

I was twelve years old, and for the first time I realised that I would be staying there for ever. My mother had died four years earlier and Mauricia, the old nanny who had looked after me, was now an invalid. My grandmother was going to take charge of me for ever, that was clear.

The day I arrived on the island, it was very windy in the city. Some placards hanging loose were rattling on the doors of the shops. Grandmother took me to a gloomy hotel that smelt of dampness and bleach. My room overlooked a small yard on one side, and on the other side, an alley at the end of which one could see a promenade with palm trees swaying over a leaden sea. The intricate design of the wrought-iron bed frightened me like an unknown animal. Grandmother was sleeping in the room next to mine and at dawn I woke up startled, as I often did, and I stretched out my arm groping for the switch of the bedside lamp. I remember well the coldness of the stuccoed wall and the pink lamp-shade. I remained very still, sitting up in bed, looking around me suspiciously, fascinated by a curly lock of my hair resting darkly on my shoulder. As I got used to the dimness I noticed, one by one, the chips on the wall, the large stains on the ceiling and, above all, the twisted shadows of the bed, like snakes, dragons or mysterious figures that I hardly dared look at. I leant over to the bedside table, to pick up a glass of water, and then, in the corner of the room, I discovered a row of ants climbing up the wall. I dropped the glass, which broke, and sunk back between the sheets, covering my head. I did not dare show even one hand and I remained that way a long time, biting my lips and trying to hold back the despicable tears. I think I was afraid. Perhaps I thought that I was completely alone, and I was looking for something I did not know.

El Coronel no tiene quien le escriba

El viernes siguiente volvió a las lanchas. Y como todos los viernes regresó a su casa sin la carta esperada. 'Ya hemos cumplido con esperar', le dijo esa noche su mujer. 'Se necesita tener esa paciencia de buey que tú tienes para esperar una carta durante quince años'. El coronel se metió en la hamaca a leer los periódicos.
–Hay que esperar el turno – dijo –. Nuestro número es el mil ochocientos veintitrés.
–Desde que estamos esperando, ese número ha salido dos veces en la lotería – replicó la mujer.

El coronel leyó, como siempre, desde la primera página hasta la última, incluso los avisos. Pero esta vez no se concentró. Durante la lectura pensó en su pensión de veterano. Diecinueve años antes, cuando el congreso promulgó la ley, se inició un proceso de justificación que duró ocho años. Luego necesitó seis años más para hacerse incluir en el escalafón. Esa fue la última carta que recibió el coronel.

Terminó después del toque de queda. Cuando iba a apagar la lámpara cayó en la cuenta de que su mujer estaba despierta.
– ¿Tienes todavía aquel recorte?

La mujer pensó.
–Sí. Debe estar con los otros papeles.

Salió del mosquitero y extrajo del armario un cofre de madera con un paquete de cartas ordenadas por las fechas y aseguradas con una cinta elástica. Localizó un anuncio de una agencia de abogados que se comprometía a una gestión activa de las pensiones de guerra.
–Desde que estoy con el tema de que cambies de abogado ya hubiéramos tenido tiempo hasta de gastarnos la plata – dijo la mujer, entregando a su marido el recorte de periódico –. Nada sacamos con que nos la metan en el cajón como a los indios.

El coronel leyó el recorte fechado dos años antes. Lo guardó en el bolsillo de la camisa colgada detrás de la puerta.
–Lo malo es que para el cambio de abogado se necesita dinero.
–Nada de eso – decidió la mujer –. Se les escribe diciendo que descuenten lo que sea de la misma pensión cuando la cobren. Es la única manera de que se interesen en el asunto.

Así que el sábado en la tarde el coronel fue a visitar a su abogado.

Taken from the novel 'El Coronel no tiene quien le escriba' by the Colombian author Gabriel García Márquez (born 1928).

No one writes to the Colonel

The following Friday he went down to the launches again. And, as on every Friday, he returned home without the long-awaited letter. 'We've waited long enough,' his wife told him that night. 'One must have the patience of an ox, as you do, to wait for a letter for fifteen years.' The colonel got into his hammock to read the newspapers.

'We have to wait our turn,' he said. 'Our number is 1823.'

'Since we've been waiting, that number has come up twice in the lottery,' his wife replied.

The colonel read, as usual, from the first page to the last, including the advertisements. But this time he didn't concentrate. During his reading, he thought about his veteran's pension. Nineteen years earlier, when Congress passed the law, it took him eight years to prove his claim. Then it took him six more years to get himself included on the rolls. That was the last letter the colonel had received.

He finished after curfew sounded. When he went to turn off the lamp, he realized that his wife was awake.

'Do you still have that clipping?'

The woman thought.

'Yes. It must be with the other papers.'

She got out of her mosquito netting and took a wooden box out of the wardrobe, with a bundle of letters arranged by dates and held together by a rubber band. She found the advertisement of a legal firm which promised quick action on war pensions.

'We could have spent the money in the time I've wasted trying to convince you to change lawyers,' the woman said, handing her husband the newspaper clipping. 'We won't get anything out of it if they put the money in our coffin as they do with the Indians.'

The colonel read the clipping dated two years before. He put it in the pocket of his jacket which was hanging behind the door.

'The problem is that to change lawyers you need money.'

'Not at all,' said the woman decisively. 'You write to them telling them to discount whatever it may be from the pension itself when they collect it. It's the only way they'll work with interest on the case.'

So, Saturday afternoon the colonel went to see his lawyer.

Un pueblo de sueño

Llegamos a Sevilla y fuimos a un hotel de una plaza con grandes palmeras.

Nos han instalado en habitaciones del piso bajo, cuyas ventanas dan a un gran patio con una fuente en medio, enlozado de mármol blanco, y rodeado de una arcada también de mármol.

El cuarto me ha parecido húmedo y frío, como sitio donde no entra el sol y que no tiene chimenea ni nada para calentarlo.

Mi marido y yo cenamos a las ocho, y después de cenar fuimos a dar una vuelta por el pueblo.

En la calle de las Sierpes he llamado la atención. ¿Por qué? Realmente no llevaba nada llamativo. Quiza encontraban en mí cierto aire exótico.

Dimos varias vueltas a esta calle estrecha tortuosa, y luego nos sentamos en un café.

Al extranjero que viene a Sevilla lo que le choca primero son los muchos hombres que andan por la calle y las pocas mujeres.

En España he oído decir que se considera a las mujeres de Sevilla como muy bonitas, pero a mí, si tengo que decir la verdad y juzgar por las de la calle, no me han llamada la atención. En el Norte y en Madrid he visto tipos más bellos y con el mismo carácter meridional.

Realmente, en España no hay gran diferencia entre la gente del Norte y la del Sur; no pasa como en Italia; aquí, por lo que veo, apenas se distingue un andaluz de un vascongado y un gallego de un catalán.

Desde la ventana del café veo, un poco cansada, como se agita la multitud de hombres que llenan la calle. Hay muchos que deben de ser toreros, porque llevan coleta como los chinos, una coleta pequeña retorcida para arriba que parece el rabito de un cerdo.

Entre algunas de estas caras anémicas, borrosas, de poca expresión, hay tipos de hombres altos, con aire enérgico, que me recuerdan las esculturas romanas del Museo de Florencia. Muchos se apoyan en las paredes en actitud de languidez y de pereza.

–¿Estás cansada o damos otro paseo? – me ha preguntado Juan.

–No, vamos.

Hemos salido del café. Son cerca de las diez de la noche y muchas tiendas están abiertas. Sigue el eterno ir y venir de la gente.

Taken and adapted from the novel 'El mundo es ansí' by Pío Baroja (1872–1956).

A dream town

We arrived in Seville and went to a hotel in a square with big palm trees.

They put us in rooms on the ground floor, whose windows overlook a large inner court with a fountain in the middle, a white marble floor and surrounded by a marble arcade.

The room seemed to me damp and cold, a place where the sun never enters and which has no fireplace or anything to warm it up.

My husband and I had dinner at eight, and after dinner we went for a walk around the town.

In Sierpes Street people were looking at me. Why? I was not wearing anything showy. Perhaps they found something exotic about me.

We walked up and down this narrow, winding street, and then went to sit in a cafe.

The first thing that strikes the foreigner who comes to Seville is how many men there are in the streets and how few women.

I have heard in Spain that the women of Seville are very pretty, but if I am to tell the truth and judge from the ones in the streets, they don't appeal to me. I have seen in the North and in Madrid much better looking women, with the same Southern characteristics.

Indeed, in Spain there is no great difference between the people of the North and that of the South; not like in Italy; here, as far as I can see, one can hardly tell an Andalusian from a Basque and a Galician from a Catalan.

From the window of the cafe I watch, feeling a little tired, the crowds of men that fill the street. Many of them must be bullfighters because they wear a plait like the Chinese, a small plait turned upwards that looks like a pig's tail.

Among these anaemic, blurred, expressionless faces, there are some tall, energetic looking men, who remind me of the Roman sculptures in the Museum in Florence. Many others are leaning against the wall in an attitude of listlessness and indolence.

'Are you tired or shall we go for another walk?' Juan asked me.

'No, let's go'.

We leave the cafe. It's nearly ten o'clock and many shops are still open. The continuous to-ing and fro-ing of people goes on.

Key to Exercises & Drills

LESSON 1

Exercise 1: 1 los libros. 2 las casas. 3 las mujeres. 4 los hombres.
5 las calles. 6 las flores. 7 los jardines. 8 los coches. 9 las
capitales. 10 las ciudades. 11 las luces. 12 las leyes.

Exercise 2: 1 los. 2 el. 3 las. 4 la. 5 el. 6 los. 7 el. 8 la. 9 el.
10 las. 11 el. 12 el.

Exercise 2 (indefinite articles): 1 unos; 2 un; 3 unas; 4 una;
5 un; 6 unos; 7 un; 8 una; 9 un; 10 unas; 11 un; 12 un.

Exercise 3: 1 el libro. 2 la mesa. 3 los billetes. 4 unos árboles.
5 una cerveza. 6 el coche. 7 una ciudad. 8 unos cigarrillos. 9 el
jardín. 10 una calle. 11 unas mujeres. 12 la estación.

Exercise 4: 1 tienen una casa. 2 no tenemos café. 3 el hombre tiene
miedo. 4 tengo que trabajar. ¿tienes un lápiz? 6 no tienen sed.
7 ¿tienen Vds. todo? 8 tengo calor. 9 tenemos que salir. 10 tiene un
hijo.

Drill 1: 1 no, no tengo hambre. 2 no, no tenemos cerveza. 3 no, no
tengo sed. 4 no, no tenemos calor. 5 no, no tengo frío. 6 no, no
tenemos los libros. 7 no, no tengo cigarrillos. 8 no, no tenemos los
billetes.

LESSON 2

Exercise 5: 1 a la iglesia. 2 del idioma. 3 al coche. 4 a la mesa. 5 de
los árboles. 6 a la casa. 7 del hombre. 8 de la ciudad. 9 a la
calle. 10 del vino. 11 al policía. 12 de la estación.

Exercise 6: 1 buenos. 2 encantadora. 3 útiles. 4 blancas.
5 barato. 6 larga. 7 altos. 8 interesantes. 9 inglés. 10 alemana.

Exercise 7: 1 son. 2 está. 3 son. 4 es. 5 están. 6 está. 7 es. 8 es.
9 está. 10 estoy.

Exercise 8: 1 es italiana. 2 las manzanas están en la cocina. 3 el
autobús está allí. 4 Madrid es la capital de España. 5 la chica es
alta. 6 la casa está en la colina. 7 es peligroso fumar. 8 el café está
demasiado dulce. 9 mañana es domingo. 10 están en la playa.

LESSON 3

Exercise 9: 1 ese coche es caro. 2 esos cigarrillos son fuertes. 3 esa iglesia es muy vieja. 4 estos amigos son de Málaga. 5 esta mesa está ocupada. 6 ese hombre está libre. 7 este ascensor está lleno. 8 esas uvas están agrias. 9 aquellos libros son interesantes. 10 es aquella playa.

Exercise 10: 1 estos, ésos. 2 esa, aquélla. 3 estas, ésas. 4 ese, éste. 5 este, aquél. 6 esos, éstos. 7 este, ése. 8 ese, éste. 9 estas, ésas. 10 este, aquél.

Exercise 11: 1 compro. 2 fuma. 3 Vd. bebe. 4 escribimos. 5 aprenden. 6 estudio. 7 hablas. 8 come. 9 vivimos. 10 suben. 11 aprendo. 12 bebe.

Exercise 12: 1 compra un periódico. 2 ¿bebe cerveza? 3 Pedro vive en Barcelona. 4 escribo a Conchita. 5 ¿estudias inglés? 6 estos niños aprenden español. 7 come demasiado. 8 subimos la colina. 9 hablo inglés. 10 fuman cigarrillos baratos.

Exercise 13: 1 el pueblo en el que vivimos. 2 la mujer que trabaja en la tienda. 3 el libro que tengo que leer. 4 la ciudad de la que estamos hablando. 5 es Pedro quien es médico. 6 ¿de quién son estas cartas? 7 ¿qué revista está comprando? 8 la casa que tiene una puerta verde. 9 la pluma con la que escribo. 10 ¿cuál es el número?

Drill 2: 1 sí, bebemos cerveza. 2 sí, como pan. 3 sí, vivimos en Londres. 4 sí, soy médico. 5 sí, hablamos español. 6 sí, compro la revista.

Drill 3: 1 no, no vivo en Barcelona. 2 no, no fumamos. 3 no, no aprendo alemán. 4 no, no compramos los periódicos. 5 no, no bebo vino. 6 no, no somos españoles.

Drill 4: 1 está comprando. 2 están bebiendo. 3 estoy estudiando. 4 estamos comiendo. 5 está leyendo. 6 estoy fumando. 7 estamos hablando. 8 está escribiendo. 9 están aprendiendo. 10 estoy subiendo.

LESSON 4

Exercise 14: 1 mi marido. 2 su hermano. 3 nuestra hermana. 4 su sobrino. 5 su tío. 6 mis padres. 7 tu mujer. 8 sus hijos. 9 su primo. 10 sus parientes.

Exercise 15: 1 la tuya. 2 el suyo. 3 el nuestro. 4 la suya. 5 la nuestra. 6 el mío. 7 la suya. 8 los vuestros. 9 la mía. 10 el suyo.

Exercise 16: 1 diez casas. 2 setenta y dos pesetas. 3 doscientos cigarrillos. 4 dieciséis cartas. 5 ciento treinta y cinco libros. 6 cuarenta y seis hoteles. 7 trescientas cincuenta y cuatro manzanas. 8 sesenta y ocho tiendas. 9 mil cuatrocientos hombres. 10 setecientos ochenta y cinco coches.

Exercise 17: 1 el séptimo libro. 2 la primera mujer. 3 la tercera hija. 4 el sexto cigarrillo. 5 la segunda puerta. 6 el décimo día. 7 la cuarta calle. 8 el noveno niño. 9 el quinto hombre. 10 la octava tienda.

Exercise 18: 1 ¿qué hora es? 2 son las diez y veinte en mi reloj. 3 trabajo hasta las once y media. 4 el invierno en Madrid es frío. 5 tienen sus vacaciones en julio. 6 mi cumpleaños es el tres de enero. 7 está libre los sábados. 8 octubre es generalmente un mes bonito. 9 tenemos que ir a Barcelona en mayo. 10 los domingos ceno con mis padres.

LESSON 5

Exercise 19: 1 vamos a la iglesia los domingos. 2 voy a comprar ese libro. 3 va a casa de su amigo. 4 vamos de vacaciones en el verano. 5 van a Madrid en tren. 6 vamos a tomar un café. 7 no va a cantar. 8 mañana voy a descansar. 9 van de compras en el mercado. 10 vamos al teatro.

Exercise 20: 1 he escrito tres cartas. 2 han hablado en español. 3 hemos comido demasiado. 4 hay azúcar en este té. 5 ha comprado un vestido nuevo. 6 ¿has terminado el trabajo?. 7 nunca ha ayudado en la casa. 8 hay unas naranjas en la bolsa. 9 ¿ ha bebido Vd. la cerveza? 10 no he visto la película.

Exercise 21: 1 a. 2 a. 3 –. 4 al. 5 –. 6 a. 7 –. 8 –. 9 –. 10 a.

Exercise 22: 1 visita a su madre. 2 he visto a la mujer. 3 tenemos que llamar a los niños. 4 María prepara la comida. 5 han invitado a sus amigos. 6 tiene una hermana casada. 7 voy a comprar un caballo. 8 tenemos que bañar al perro. 9 están esperando al profesor. 10 Carlos no ha visto Toledo.

Exercise 23: 1 Juan se lo ofrece; 2 la bebo por la mañana; 3 lo hemos comprado; 4 me las ha enviado; 5 se la he escrito; 6 los comemos; 7 estos señores no lo comprenden; 8 tengo que estudiarla; 9 nos las ha vendido; 10 se los hemos dado.

Exercise 24: 1 no fume Vd. esos cigarrillos. 2 beba Vd. este vino. 3 envíeme Vd. la revista. 4 léales Vd. la carta. 5 véndale Vd. su reloj. 6 aprenda Vd. estos números. 7 escriba Vd. su nombre aquí. 8 no coma Vd. esas manzanas. 9 no compre Vd. esa carne. 10 no me los dé Vd.

Exercise 24 (plurals): 1 no fumen Vds. 2 beban Vds. 3 envíenme Vds. 4 léanles Vds. 5 véndanle Vds. 6 aprendan Vds. 7 escriban Vds. 8 no coman Vds. 9 no compren Vds. 10 no me los den Vds.

Drill 5: 1 no, voy a tomarla ahora. 2 no, van a ir ahora. 3 no, va a escribirla ahora. 4 no, vamos a hacerlo ahora. 5 no, voy a comprarlos ahora. 6 no, van a verle ahora. 7 no, vamos a terminarla ahora. 8 no, va a llamarla ahora. 9 no, voy a subirlas ahora. 10 no, vamos a beberlo ahora.

Drill 6: 1 sí, cómprelo. 2 sí, súbanlas. 3 sí, llámele. 4 sí, invítenles. 5 sí, léala. 6 sí, envíenlas. 7 sí, bébala. 8 sí, véndanla.

Drill 7: 1 ya lo he preparado. 2 ya le hemos llamado. 3 ya lo he escrito. 4 ya la hemos tomado. 5 ya los he comprado. 6 ya les hemos hablado. 7 ya los he contado. 8 ya lo hemos vendido. 9 ya la he leído.

LESSON 6

Exercise 25: 1 Pedro y Anita se escriben todos los días. 2 el coche va a pararse. 3 vamos a casarnos. 4 los niños se acuestan a las ocho. 5 tenemos que lavarnos. 6 los dos hombres se odian. 7 siempre me pide dinero. 8 nunca se ayudan. 9 Carlos vuelve de la oficina a las seis y media. 10 tengo que dormirme. 11 llévese Vd. estas tazas. 12 la calle se llama Baeza. 13 voy a sentarme aquí. 14 nos vamos mañana. 15 me he decidido a vivir en España.

Exercise 26: 1 estamos trabajando con ellos. 2 ha comprado un regalo para mí. 3 ¿va a volver con Vd.? 4 el tiempo está contra nosotros. 5 se han ido sin él. 6 siempre ha vivido conmigo. 7 estas cartas son para ella. 8 van a comprar la casa entre ellos. 9 ¿están los niños contigo? 10 según él, el viaje es demasiado largo.

Exercise 27: 1 ¿qué tiempo hace? 2 hoy hace mucho frío. 3 va a llover mañana. 4 no me gusta esta cerveza. 5 va a traernos café. 6 le

gusta salir todas las tardes. 7 no sé dondé está. 8 van a España
porque les gusta el sol. 9 hace veinticinco años. 10 a Carmen le
gusta sentarse en el jardín.

Drill 8: 1 sí, me gusta mucho. 2 sí, le gustan mucho. 3 sí, nos gusta
mucho. 4 sí, nos gusta mucho. 5 sí, le gusta mucho. 6 sí, me gustan
mucho. 7 sí, me gusta mucho. 8 sí, les gusta mucho. 9 sí, nos gusta
mucho. 10 sí, les gusta mucho.

Drill 9: 1 sí, trabajo con ella. 2 sí, es para Vds. 3 sí, vuelve
conmigo. 4 sí, vamos sin ellos. 5 sí, son para Vd. 6 sí, vive con
ellos. 7 sí, son para nosotros. 8 sí, voy sin él.

Drill 10: 1 sí, quisiera sentarme. 2 sí, quisiera lavarme. 3 sí,
quisiera dormirme. 4 sí, quisiera irme. 5 sí, quisiera pararme. 6 sí,
quisiéramos sentarnos. 7 sí, quisiéramos lavarnos. 8 sí, quisiéramos
dormirnos. 9 sí, quisiéramos irnos. 10 sí, quisiéramos pararnos.

LESSON 7

Exercise 28: 1 Luis fumaba un cigarrillo. 2 generalmente la veo por
la mañana. 3 habían hablado con el gerente del hotel. 4 solía
traerme bombones. 5 el muchacho buscaba su maleta. 6 la
representación solía empezar a las diez. 7 había trabajado en una
fábrica. 8 el mar estaba muy frío. 9 la mujer nos miraba.
10 solíamos comer mucho pescado.

Exercise 29: 1 nada. 2 nadie. 3 ni, ni. 4 nunca. 5 ningún.
6 tampoco. 7 nadie. 8 nada. 9 ninguna. 10 nunca.

Exercise 30: 1 felizmente. 2 verdaderamente. 3 tristemente.
4 lentamente. 5 nuevamente. 6 agradablemente. 7 malamente.
8 ciertamente. 9 rápidamente. 10 claramente.

Exercise 31: 1 mi hermano es más fuerte que yo. 2 este jerez es más
seco que ése. 3 Carlos es tres años mayor que María. 4 los zapatos
negros son más pequeños que los azules. 5 su coche es mejor que el
mío. 6 escribe peor que su hermana. 7 he llegado más pronto que
mi padre. 8 no tienen tanto dinero como sus amigos. 9 no necesito
tantas maletas como tú. 10 el agua en la piscina está más caliente que
en el mar.

Drill 11: 1 sí, solía verla. 2 sí, solían comer. 3 sí, solíamos
trabajar. 4 sí, solía escribirlas. 5 sí, solía viajar. 6 sí, solíamos ir.
7 sí, solía hablarlo. 8 sí, solía invitarles. 9 sí, solían tenerlo. 10 sí,
solía beberlo.

Drill 12: 1 no, no quiero nada.   2 no, no han vivido aquí nunca.
3 no, no queremos ni té ni café.   4 no, no hay ningún turista inglés.
5 no, no conocemos a nadie.   6 no, no tengo ninguna revista
española.

Drill 13: 1 los míos son más viejos.   2 el mío es peor.   3 el mío es más
bonito.   4 el mío es mejor.   5 el mío es más alto.   6 los míos son más
caros.   7 las mías son más grandes.   8 los míos son más baratos.

LESSON 8

Exercise 32: 1 hemos tenido un buen viaje.   2 cada hombre tenía un
trabajo.   3 es un gran pintor.   4 siempre llevan la misma ropa.   5 hay
bastantes hoteles en esta zona.   6 la pobre mujer ha perdido su
bolso.   7 tengo un sombrero nuevo.   8 hemos pedido otra bebida.
9 estos sellos son muy viejos.   10 todos los niños son buenos
nadadores.

Exercise 33: 1 se casarán el próximo mes.   2 me acostaré temprano
esta noche.   3 vendrá con nosotros de vacaciones.   4 les visitaremos el
domingo.   5 no quieren hablar con nosotros.   6 sería mejor parar.
7 no me gustaría conducir un coche grande.   8 no tendrá que andar
muy lejos.   9 no valdrían nada.   10 no podremos ver el museo.   11 no
quería vender la casa.   12 el autocar saldrá a las ocho.

Exercise 34: 1 cierre Vd. las ventanas antes de acostarse.   2 tendré
que pensar antes de decidir.   3 no puedes irte antes de terminar el
trabajo.   4 ha pasado el día sin hablar con nadie.   5 lloraba sin saber
por qué.   6 se sentían enfermos después de comer marisco.   7 tenía
mucho sueño después de trabajar toda la noche.   8 nos gustaría ver la
habitación antes de tomarla.   9 su voz estaba ronca de gritar
tanto.   10 después de escribir la carta enséñemela Vd.

Drill 14: 1 no, le verán luego.   2 no, lo terminaremos luego.   3 no, iré
luego.   4 no, la escribirá luego.   5 no, las enviaremos luego.   6 no, la
cerrarán luego.   7 no, saldrá luego.   8 no, la haré luego.   9 no, las
verán luego.   10 no, las abriré luego.

Drill 15: 1 hace seis meses que estudio español.   2 hace tres años
que estamos en Madrid.   3 hace dos semanas que trabajan aquí.
4 hace un año que vive en Londres.   5 hace diez minutos que espero.
6 llevo seis meses estudiando español.   7 llevamos tres años en
Madrid.   8 llevan dos semanas trabajando aquí.   9 lleva un año
viviendo en Londres.   10 llevo diez minutos esperando.

LESSON 9

Exercise 35: 1 dimos un paseo por el río. 2 no quisieron verme.
3 puse la carta en el sobre. 4 murió dos años después. 5 pagó la
comida con un cheque. 6 el camarero nos trajo las bebidas y se fue.
7 anduvieron cinco kilómetros buscando un garaje. 8 salí a las diez y
volví a la hora de comer. 9 le dijimos que su padre había llegado.
10 no hizo nada toda la mañana.

Exercise 36: 1 salió. 2 estaba, sonó. 3 viajaban, tuvieron.
4 jugaban, empezó. 5 bajó, hacía. 6 se sentaba. 7 volví. 8 hacía,
llegamos. 9 recibió, vivía. 10 preguntó.

Exercise 37: 1 no conocen ese disco. 2 sabe que quiero un
tocadiscos. 3 ese programa de televisión es divertidísimo. 4 esta
talla es la más pequeña que tenemos. 5 estos zapatos son los más
bonitos, ésos son los más baratos. 6 es el hombre más amable que
conozco. 7 no saben que deseo verles. 8 fue una conversación
interesantísima. 9 es la iglesia más vieja de esta ciudad. 10 la
farmacia estaba lejísimos de la parada de autobús.

Exercise 38: 1 el té es una bebida muy agradable. 2 la señora
Collado llegará el domingo. 3 se puso los guantes porque hacía
frío. 4 él es camarero y ella es dependienta. 5 pasé dos semanas en el
hospital. 6 lo importante es no preocuparse. 7 la pobre María se ha
roto el brazo derecho. 8 los libros son muy caros hoy día. 9 andaba
con gran dificultad. 10 va a traer otra taza. 11 bebimos media
botella de coñac. 12 lo mejor es vender la casa.

Drill 16: 1 pero tuvo que escribirla. 2 pero tuvieron que pagarla.
3 pero tuve que verle. 4 pero tuvimos que ir. 5 pero tuvo que salir.
6 pero tuvo que hacerla. 7 pero tuvo que comerlo. 8 pero tuvo que
fumarlo. 9 pero tuve que dárselo. 10 pero tuvimos que beberla.

Drill 17: 1 no, estuvimos ayer. 2 no, vinieron ayer. 3 no, lo compré
ayer. 4 no, la pagaron ayer. 5 no, la recibió ayer. 6 no, las hicimos
ayer. 7 no, llovió ayer. 8 no, las trajeron ayer. 9 no, fuimos
ayer. 10 no, les visité ayer.

Drill 18: 1 sí, es el más bonito que he visto. 2 sí, son los más caros
que he visto. 3 sí, es la más grande que he visto. 4 sí, es el más
elegante que he visto. 5 sí, son los más divertidos que he visto. 6 sí,
son las más pequeñas que he visto.

LESSON 10

Exercise 39: 1 por. 2 por. 3 para. 4 por. 5 para. 6 para. 7 por. 8 para. 9 para. 10 por.

Exercise 40: 1 tenemos que pasar por la Aduana. 2 nos cobraron dos mil pesetas por la comida. 3 es demasiado tarde para ir al cine. 4 necesito una bolsa para todas mis compras. 5 ¿tiene Vd. una llave para abrir este armario? 6 este libro es demasiado difícil para él. 7 el avión sale para Madrid a las siete y cuarto. 8 haría cualquier cosa por él. 9 leímos la carta por curiosidad. 10 quiere comprar unos melocotones para su madre.

Exercise 41: 1 la casa fue construída por su abuelo. 2 fui acusado del robo. 3 el barco se vendió por ochenta mil pesetas. 4 el trabajo está terminado ahora. 5 se cree que está muerto. 6 las montañas estaban cubiertas de nieve. 7 la cena no se sirve hasta las nueve. 8 las ventanas se pintaron hace tres semanas. 9 fueron recibidos por uno de los directores. 10 el programa fue presentado por un famoso actor.

Exercise 42: 1 jugué con los niños toda la tarde. 2 están construyendo un aparcamiento nuevo. 3 oyó un ruido arriba. 4 me sequé los pies al fuego. 5 cayeron al suelo. 6 está leyendo las instrucciones. 7 huyeron de España al principio de la guerra. 8 pagué mucho dinero por ese cuadro. 9 coja Vd. el equipaje, por favor. 10 creyó que la tienda estaba cerrada.

Exercise 43: 1 conseguí hablar con ellos. 2 nos aconsejó alquilar un coche. 3 trataron de entrar en la habitación. 4 pienso quejarme del servicio. 5 estamos aprendiendo a jugar al tenis. 6 volví a llamarle. 7 el señor Solís acaba de llegar. 8 se cansó de subir y se sentó. 9 dejó de llover y salió el sol. 10 me olvidé de darle el recado. 11 insistieron en pagar sus billetes. 12 el paquete tardó dos semanas en llegar. 13 acabaron por tener una discusión. 14 la mujer se esforzó por sonreír. 15 el hombre amenazó con llamar a la policía. 16 se contenta con ganar muy poco.

Drill 19: 1 para. 2 por. 3 para. 4 para. 5 por. 6 para. 7 para. 8 por.

Drill 20: 1 el libro se publicó. 2 los coches se alquilaron. 3 la puerta se abrió. 4 los ruidos se oyeron. 5 el trabajo se terminó. 6 la casa se construyó. 7 los barcos se vendieron. 8 la carta se leyó.

156

Drill 21: 1 sí, acabo de comprarlos. 2 sí, acaban de llegar. 3 sí, acabo de recibirlas. 4 sí, acabamos de hacerlas. 5 sí, acaban de acostarse. 6 sí, acabo de encontrarla.

LESSON 11

Exercise 44: 1 ¿cuánto le debo? 2 no deberían decir esas cosas. 3 debe de tener un buen trabajo. 4 debo ver a un médico. 5 ¿sabe hablar español? 6 no puedo leer sin gafas. 7 deberíamos ir allí más a menudo. 8 me debe una explicación. 9 esa sortija debe de costar mucho dinero. 10 no sé montar en bicicleta. 11 no puede dormir sin tomar píldoras. 12 ¿sabe Vd. guisar?.

Exercise 45: 1 me alegro de que puedan venir. 2 quiere que el abogado vea los documentos. 3 nos han mandado que esperemos aquí. 4 dudo que salga el sol. 5 me sorprende que no haya escrito. 6 me ha pedido que le enseñe español. 7 es posible que se hayan perdido. 8 es una lástima que no tengamos bastante dinero. 9 es probable que se casen. 10 no podré hacerlo a no ser que me ayuden. 11 iremos al cine con tal que me dejes pagar. 12 esperará hasta que yo vuelva. 13 tendrán que comerlo, aunque no les guste. 14 no hay nadie que pueda pagar ese precio. 15 ¿hay alguien que sepa tocar el piano? 16 necesito una mujer que cuide de los niños. 17 lo encontraremos, dondequiera que esté. 18 te ayudará cuandoquiera que tengas un problema. 19 por mucho que trate, nunca tendrá éxito. 20 por muy fácil que parezca, se necesita práctica.

Exercise 46: 1 hazlo, no lo hagas, hacedlo, no lo hagáis. 2 ven, no vengas, venid, no vengáis. 3 acuéstate, no te acuestes, acostaos, no os acostéis. 4 aprende, no aprendas, aprended, no aprendáis. 5 ponlo, no lo pongas, ponedlo, no lo pongáis. 6 escríbela, no la escribas, escribidla, no la escribáis. 7 grita, no grites, gritad, no gritéis. 8 óyelo, no lo oigas. oídlo, no lo oigáis. 9 preocúpate, no te preocupes, preocupaos, no os preocupéis. 10 duérmete, no te duermas, dormíos, no os durmáis.

Exercise 47: 1 no te enfades. 2 escuchadme. 3 vístete. 4 no me digáis eso. 5 tened cuidado. 6 léenoslo. 7 callaos. 8 no me despiertes temprano. 9 perdonad mi error. 10 no muevas el coche.

Drill 22: 1 sí, debe de estar enfermo. 2 sí, deben de ser las cinco. 3 sí, deben de estar muy tristes. 4 sí, debe de trabajar mucho. 5 sí, debe de hacer muchos años. 6 sí, deben de estar en casa.

Drill 23: 1 sí, es preferible que coman. 2 sí, es preferible que se vaya. 3 sí, es preferible que volvamos. 4 sí, es preferible que se acuesten. 5 sí, es preferible que pague. 6 sí, es preferible que nos sentemos.

Drill 24: 1 sí, pedidlos. 2 sí, tráelo. 3 sí, llamadle. 4 sí, cómpralo. 5 sí, abridlas. 6 sí, ayúdale.

Drill 25: 1 no, siguen comiendo. 2 no, sigue leyéndolo. 3 no, seguimos trabajando. 4 no, sigo pintando. 5 no, sigue cantando. 6 no, siguen construyéndola.

LESSON 12

Exercise 48: 1 querían que viajase con ellos. 2 tenía miedo de que hubiera tenido un accidente. 3 nos dijo que pusiéramos la mesa. 4 le pedí que se diera prisa. 5 esperábamos que no hiciese demasiado calor en Sevilla. 6 dondequiera que fuese, siempre encontraba amigos. 7 le avisé que no usara esa máquina. 8 me llamó por teléfono para que reservara las habitaciones. 9 buscaban a una persona que pudiese traducir la carta. 10 me alegro de que ganaran el primer premio.

Exercise 49: 1 lo haría si pudiera. 2 si hace buen tiempo, trabajaré en el jardín. 3 el perro no te habría mordido si no le hubieses pegado. 4 si les preguntaras, no sabrían que decir. 5 si le viera ahora, no le hablaría. 6 Vd. no habría perdido el dinero, si lo hubiera guardado en su bolsillo. 7 si vinieran a la fiesta, se divertirían. 8 te escribiré, si tengo que quedarme allí más tiempo. 9 si no llevas un paraguas, te mojarás. 10 yo iría al concierto, si él viniera conmigo.

Exercise 50: 1 ojalá no tuviera que trabajar. 2 quizá esté enfermo. 3 puede que haya perdido el tren. 4 que venga, si quiere. 5 ojalá pudiéramos tener unas vacaciones. 6 pase lo que pase, estaré en contacto con Vd. 7 ¿podemos ver las fotografías? 8 dijo que yo podía tener el día libre. 9 ¡que se divierta Vd! 10 quizá no vieran el aviso.

Exercise 51: 1 no te acerques al borde. 2 se asomó a la ventanilla del coche. 3 mi hermano va a casarse con una chica inglesa; 4 sabes que puedes contar conmigo. 5 la ventana daba a una calle muy concurrida. 6 el éxito de la obra depende de los actores. 7 tengo que despedirme de mis compañeros. 8 no dudan de su buena intención. 9 María se ha enamorado de un hombre muy tonto. 10 es muy fácil encontrarse con turistas ingleses en España. 11 no hemos podido enterarnos de su nombre. 12 no me fijé en lo que llevaba. 13 tienes que ocuparte de las bebidas. 14 esta casa se parece mucho a la nuestra. 15 no quiere pensar en todos los problemas. 16 no sabemos lo que piensa de la situación. 17 este helado sabe a fresa. 18 soñaba con todos los lugares que había visitado.

Drill 26: 1 puede que lo venda. 2 puede que se casen. 3 puede que salgamos. 4 puede que vuelva. 5 puede que nos inviten. 6 puede que nade.

Drill 27: 1 vendrían si pudieran. 2 lo pediríamos si lo necesitaramos. 3 comería si tuviera hambre. 4 se lo diríamos si le viéramos. 5 saldrían si no lloviera. 6 te lo daría si lo encontrara. 7 trabajaría más si le pagaran bien. 8 hablaría con ellos si vinieran.

Drill 28: 1 se sorprendió al oír la noticia. 2 gritaron al ver a los policías. 3 lloraba al leer la carta. 4 me pidió la llave al salir. 5 tuve miedo al oír un ruido. 6 se lavaron las manos al terminar. 7 me quité el sombrero al entrar. 8 empezó a llover al llegar a casa.

LESSON 13

Exercise 52: 1 mucha gente asistió al entierro. 2 esta cantidad de harina bastará. 3 esa caja no cabe en el maletero. 4 quiero devolver la revista que me prestó. 5 echó la pelota a los niños. 6 voy a echar el vino. 7 les falta experiencia. 8 faltan cinco libros de este estante. 9 nos hacen falta más ayudantes. 10 meterán toda la ropa en una maleta. 11 ¿cuántos días te quedan? 12 quitará estas sillas. 13 ¿puedo quitarme la chaqueta? 14 sobran huevos para hacer la tortilla. 15 es muy agradable tocar seda. 16 le gustaría tocar el violín. 17 tomó la pluma y firmó la carta. 18 les gusta tomar vino con su comida.

Exercise 53: 1 ha heredado más de veinte millones de pesetas. 2 no puedo venderlo por menos de diez mil pesetas. 3 hemos vivido en Madrid más de quince años. 4 lo haré en menos de cinco minutos. 5 nunca había visto un collar tan bonito. 6 ¡qué edificio tan feo! 7 no haría tal cosa. 8 encuentro tales libros muy aburridos. 9 ese no es mi hermano, sino mi primo. 10 no tienen un perro, pero tienen dos gatos. 11 tiene más dinero de lo que dice. 12 son más listos de lo que crees. 13 ¡qué idea tan buena! 14 ¡es un viaje tan largo!

Exercise 54: 1 el hombre dormía bajo un árbol. 2 me escribió desde Córdoba. 3 después del teatro, fuimos a su casa. 4 es muy espléndido con sus amigos. 5 esperamos a la puerta, pero no vino. 6 según su padre, está muy enfermo. 7 había un fila larga de coches delante de mí. 8 tuvo que presentarse ante el juez. 9 se fueron sin pagar la bebida. 10 puso la maleta debajo de la cama. 11 hay una zapatería enfrente de la panadería. 12 no te veré hasta el domingo. 13 el ascensor se paró entre los dos pisos. 14 quiero probarlo antes de comprarlo. 15 empezaremos a andar hacia la estación. 16 tendrán que ir en el autobús. 17 el libro ha caído detrás del sofá. 18 dejaré el paquete encima del escritorio.

Drill 29: 1 no, no le hace falta. 2 no, no nos hace falta. 3 no, no me hacen falta. 4 no, no les hace falta. 5 no, no le hacen falta. 6 no, no nos hace falta.

Drill 30: 1 no podemos devolverlo todavía. 2 no puedo meterla todavía. 3 no pueden echarlas todavía. 4 no puedo quitármelos todavía. 5 no podemos tomarlo todavía. 6 no puede pagarla todavía.

Drill 31: 1 hasta. 2 desde. 3 enfrente de. 4 encima de. 5 entre. 6 sin. 7 con. 8 antes de. 9 en. 10 hacia.

Index

The numbers refer to section headings, *not* pages.

160